SARA WENGER SHENK

Sara Wenger Shenk is the mother of two sons and is currently living in Illinois, USA, with her family, where she writes from home. She has lived more than half of her life in Africa and Eastern Europe, and spent her childhood in Ethiopia as the daughter of Mennonite missionary teachers. The fifth child in a family of eight, she graduated from Eastern Mennonite College in Virginia with a BA in English education. After marrying N. Gerald Shenk in 1975, she and her husband studied for two years at Fuller Theological Seminary in California.

Elaine Storkey, author of *What's Right With Feminism?* has said of *And Then There Were Three*. 'It is a tremendous book. The breadth of concern takes us further than anything similar on the English market. Its loose style will make it extremely accessible to many; the writing is immediate, urgent, warm, compassionate and involves the reader fully. Men will miss out if they don't read it. This deserves to be a bestseller.'

SPIRE

By The Same Author

Why Not Celebrate!

SPIRE

Sara Wenger Shenk

AND THEN THERE WERE THREE

An Ode to Parenthood

Copyright © 1985 by Herald Press

First published in Great Britain 1989

Spire is an imprint of Hodder & Stoughton *Publishers*

British Library Cataloguing in Publication Data

Shenk, Sara Wenger, *1953–*
And then there were three: an ode to
parenthood
1. Motherhood. Personal observations
I. Title
3068'743'0924

ISBN 0-340-50042-5

*Reproduced from the original setting by arrangement with
Herald Press*

*Printed in Great Britain for Hodder and Stoughton Limited, Mill Road, Dunton
Green, Sevenoaks, Kent by Richard Clay Limited, Bungay, Suffolk.*

Hodder and Stoughton Editorial Office: 47 Bedford Square, London WC1B 3DP.

To
Sara,
my mother and
Sara,
her mother.

Contents

II. PEDAGOGY OF PARENTHOOD

Acknowledgments

While this is my story, it is also our story. I have received abundant encouragement from family and friends during its birth. If any wisdom is mine, I owe it to those who helped to shape my understanding and aided in unraveling my perplexity.

Heartfelt thanks go to Gerald, my foremost critic and finest friend; to Charlotte and Phil Baker-Shenk who first suggested that I undertake the project and encouraged me throughout its inception; and to Juanita Epp, Reta Finger, Betty Good, Ruth Detweiler Lesher, Mark Wenger, and others who read and responded to the manuscript at various steps along the way.

And finally to editor Paul M. Schrock whose belief in the project from its beginning stages gave me the courage and momentum needed to carry through to completion.

This book is also enriched by some of my favorite writers, whose books have often given answers to my questions before I knew how to ask. I have attempted to give credit where credit is due, but am aware that their thoughts have become my thoughts in more ways than I can acknowledge. I hope that my particular synthesis of the threads of truth woven into the fabric of my story will give comfort and courage to you who read it.

Sara Wenger Shenk
Evanston, Illinois

Introduction
To Be or Not to Be "Liberated"

On a cold winter night our family was making a stressful overnight train trip from Switzerland to Yugoslavia. My husband, Gerald, was assigned to a men's sleeping compartment, with three-year-old Joseph in his charge. I had a berth in a women's compartment with Timothy, aged three months.

My two cabinmates were expecting the worst. Timothy was screaming in full fury as the journey began. I did my utmost to calm him. Frequent nursing and soothing kept him in line through border crossings, customs inspections, and a blaring radio with raucous drunken laughter in the next compartment.

As dawn began to gleam faintly ahead of us, Gerald came for Timothy to give me a break. While he paced the passageway rocking our baby, a burly fellow laughed in derision nearby.

"I never touched mine until they were at least two years old!" he scoffed.

I was standing nearby, enjoying the relief of empty arms.

For a moment I winced with guilt. His scorn was directed both at my adequacy and at Gerald's masculinity. But then a far more powerful gratitude replaced my twinge of guilt— gratitude for a husband who is man enough to care for our little ones; gratitude that I am not the slave of a man who despises babies and those who stoop to be intimately involved in their care; and gratitude that I am part of a faith community which increasingly welcomes women to exercise their gifts in the church, and encourages men to minister to the children among us.

This book emerges from my deep conviction that women and men are equal partners in life. I understand them as co-heirs both of the capability and the responsibility to serve God with their total beings.

It is not another book suggesting that we revere mothers as a supreme species of selfless persons. Nor is it a book that denigrates a mother's service and sacrifice as something a "liberated" woman should steer clear of.

It is a very personal book, written by a woman who used to think of motherhood as an unliberated thing to do, but who on becoming a mother discovered many new dimensions of liberation. My story will speak particularly to women who have struggled to balance family concerns and professional pursuits. We each move toward freedom from within our own class, race, and gender.

Liberation means so many different things to different people that I have needed to define it in terms of my personal story at the risk of considerable self-disclosure. Added to the vulnerability of this are the distractions of everyday life. I am now the mother of two very lively little boys who throw magnificent displays of fireworks to lure Mom away from the blue scribbles on her paper.

Oh for a chalet on the quiet shores of a golden pond from which to ponder my metamorphosis into motherhood! But no, the baby at my knee impatiently clamoring, and the boy at my elbow drawing zany clowns "for you, Mom" add poignancy and urgency to my reflection on this enormous upheaval in the life of any woman: motherhood.

I was present several years ago at a church celebration of Mothers' Day. Little children in the most endearing voices imaginable recited poems in honor of their mothers. Many an adult eye filled with tears. The pastor reminded the congregation of the sacrifices their mothers had made for them. Attractive bouquets of flowers had been prepared for each child to carry to his or her mother. Three-year-old Joseph bounded up gleefully, bouquet in hand, and thrust it to me. "Mama, this is for you!"

My response was mixed. It was the first time I had attended a Mothers' Day program as a mother. That Joseph would single me out of that large congregation was indeed heartwarming. But why had mothers been spoken of during the service in such reverent, teary voices? Why did the congregation feel compelled to place mothers on a sacred pedestal? Is Fathers' Day celebrated with such fanfare and teary affection? Why are women's gifts (other than motherhood) undervalued, rarely mentioned, and never exercised in that pulpit?

I gladly received Joseph's bouquet and gave him a squeeze. Then I suggested that we share it with his father and another friend beside us. He readily agreed.

Don't misunderstand me. I think motherhood is very special, and that mothers deserve to be acknowledged and appreciated far more than they actually are. But the annual burst of sentimental celebration of motherhood may only conceal a deeper attitude of pity for a mother's plight. It might even betray a secret awareness that mothers are actually being exploited.

Many indeed feel sorry for the mother who from dawn to dusk is trailed by wailing kids and tied to the drudgery of keeping a house. She can't often maintain a decent conversation about culture or current events. She does chat endlessly about her little urchins. She loses touch with her peers. Her range of vision becomes more and more restricted.

It is also easy to blame the mother herself for not using her mind well and for not pursuing a more active role in the world outside. How did she consent to reduce herself to the level of the little ones clamoring around her? For the mother left with dirty socks and diapers, the praises of her sacrifice may ring rather hollow when all others abandon her for more prestigious pursuits.

The traditional split between domestic duties for women and public privileges for men has not served women well. Contemporary Christian women especially are caught in a double bind. In one ear we hear the old understanding of a woman's role which tells us to find our fulfillment at home. In the other ear we hear some feminist rhetoric implying that mothers and homemakers are unenlightened and losing ground in the struggle toward liberation. The irony is that in attempting to break down the myth that a woman must only find her fulfillment in motherhood, the women's movement seemed to put down mothers in the process of critiquing motherhood as an institution.

How can Christian mothers chart a path through these dilemmas in their struggle to maintain personal wholeness? On my own pilgrimage I have often been inspired by the work of biblical feminists who are reconceiving the Christian vision in terms of mutuality at home, at work, and in the church. Feminism that is biblical must change the old pattern in which a woman too often gave herself entirely to her husband and children, only to be left empty and alone. Becoming a mother, and for a time primarily a homemaker, has increased my commitment to the biblical passion for just relations in the home, the church, and in society.

Feminism which is faithful to the biblical message and relevant to contemporary life encourages a change in the father's role also, urging him to move back into his children's lives and to join in full partnership with his wife. Men make a mockery of their praise for motherhood if they aren't willing to nurture children themselves and participate in the least pleasant chores of household life. The most thankless tasks become more bearable when shared. The responsibilities traditionally reserved to mothers hold valuable lessons in servanthood for all who join in them. This in turn frees mothers to look to their own needs for growth, renewal, and friendship. The benefits of nurture and good parenting can then flow among all of us, instead of just from mother to child.

For those of us who spend much time at home with children, the glamorous, child-free, go-where-you-want lifestyle of a career and profession has a strong allure. We have resisted that allure because we are committed to the work of parenting. By choosing to become parents we are saying that *helping children grow is of vital importance*. And the most exciting thing about parenting done in an atmosphere of mutuality and support is that we ourselves develop in valuable ways during the process of caring for our children.

Motherhood is a woman's issue because a woman bears the child and in our culture is usually the one who has primary care of that child. Yet motherhood (parenthood) is also a man's issue, for men are the fathers and partners.

A woman called out to Jesus, "Blessed is the womb that bore you, and the breasts that you sucked!" (Luke 11:27, RSV).

Jesus responded, "Blessed rather are those who hear the word of God and keep it!"—a word of great encouragement to those who have felt restricted by their society to expect their primary fulfillment in reproduction and nurture. But Jesus' statement is also a word of command. Performing the motherly functions of birthing and nurturing is not enough. He calls for understanding and obedience, theological awareness and witness by *all* his followers.

In some ways, motherhood means increased bondage and hardship for me. In other ways, thanks to a supportive husband and community and my clear desire to maintain a personal momentum and identity apart from my family, I am discovering motherhood to be a liberating experience far beyond my expectations.

This book is the story of my fumbling entry into motherhood, an experience central to the lives of many women, fulfilling even in its sorrows and a key to understanding life.

We all have far to go in comprehending the height, breadth, and depth of the liberty that is ours in Christ Jesus. Thank God we are on the way.

Part I
Struggle Toward Life

1

The Intimate Stranger

Awaiting Birth

"Daughters of Jerusalem, do not weep for me; weep for yourselves and for your children. For the time will come when you will say, 'Blessed are the barren women, the wombs that never bore and the breasts that never nursed!' "
—*Jesus in Luke 23:28-29*

When the doctor told me that I was indeed "with child," I didn't know whether to laugh or cry. He had only confirmed what I already suspected, but I was shaking as I hurriedly walked away from his office.

That moment of truth (verily, verily!) is a moment fraught with emotion for a mother-to-be. For some it spells pure joy after much waiting. For others it is laden with fear and trembling. For many, the emotions are mixed.

I felt ambivalent, from start to finish. On the eve of due date, when great with child, I wrote in my journal, "Now I don't know how to feel: a bit apprehensive; ready and yet never sure I am ready for the enormous changes and new responsibilities; not sure that anything *will* happen; eager and yet hesitant; almost depressed with the conflict of not feeling ready and yet tired of waiting."

No one (at least no wise one) can be absolutely sure that she is ready. But the adventure is in the daring.

It has been almost six years since Gerald and I dared. We chose to begin our family during a sojourn of work and study in Zagreb, Yugoslavia. I am amazed, looking back, that we had the nerve. The timing was right for us personally, but we little suspected the agonies of becoming parents at such distance from the counsel of our own families in Pennsylvania. The unknowns of cultural patterns and medical care systems loomed larger than we knew. But when our small one first shuddered in my womb I could only guess at the vulnerabilities just ahead.

With a helpless someone coming into being within me, I began to sense that my outlook on the world was undergoing revolutionary change. No longer could I be a solitary sojourner. Now I was bearing a child, thrusting a new person into the uncertainties, terrors, and risks of life in this world. Innocence of babes in the language of poets denotes pure joy. But in this world the innocents are too often doomed to suffer its worst indignities.

Sometimes I blissfully forget the rampant madness that fuels some 40 wars around the world, that threatens massive nuclear overkill, and that widely abuses children and rapes women. Especially on bright spring days, with birds in song and trees in blossom, I could almost believe that all was right with the world and that my unborn baby would grow up to be brave, compassionate, and alive.

I have often viewed life as a sojourn of faith in an alien

land. That sort of sojourning has us "on the way" in a kingdom where God reigns, a kingdom so just and perfect and liberated that its reality is "not of this world." But we also live and birth our babies in *this* world. Living concurrently between the two realities—God's sphere of blessing and the sphere of human selfishness—provides the sojourner with much creative tension.

I used to think reading the news is an important part of being a responsible Christian. As a prospective parent, however, I found it easier to understand why many don't read, or care, or look beyond their suburban coves. It's too tough to muster up enough faith to match the terror. We become more vulnerable to despair when we anticipate introducing a tiny, soft baby into our tenuous existence. Then how do we cope with the agony that is our world?

Can we push back the madness and create an enclave of security for our children without becoming calloused toward other people in need? Can we enable our children to feel safe in God's love without unduly sheltering them? Can we show them that their world is good while equipping them to deal with the reality of evil? Can we teach hope to our children while grasping for hope ourselves? Who would dare to try? Might not the "barren women" of whom Jesus spoke truly be more blessed than persons like myself with the dubious distinction of being "with child"? I wondered. They at least would never know the ugly fear that grips parents' hearts when their child is exposed to a life of perils and unknowns.

Even birthing seemed in the distant future, though, as I emerged from the doctor's office flushed with confirmation of my first pregnancy. The terrors out there were eclipsed for the moment by the tremors within my being. My body was undergoing irreversible changes. Yet even as I watched it swell, my concept of myself didn't grow to include "pregnant" as a self-definition.

Why then did people react to my "condition" instead of relating to me as they had before? My self-identity felt as though it were slipping. I would never be the same again, at least in the eyes of those around me. My future was being transformed. A miracle of creation was happening inside me. An explosion of life within me was out of my control. Frightening. Awesome!

Perhaps it seems that I was overreacting. After all, millions of women have survived the trauma and lead perfectly normal lives. Many thousands of babies are born every day. A horde of drippy-nosed kids nipping and yapping at each other is hardly something to marvel about. Conceiving, birthing, and raising children is commonplace and very everyday, is it not?

Indeed it is! But you can talk with such nonchalance only until *you* are pregnant; until *your* automatic systems go into gear to produce another unique embodiment of God's image; until *you*, somebody's child, become overnight somebody's parent! To give birth is at once very everyday *and* absolutely profound. Its impact is very personal and deeply felt.

"All human life on the planet is born of woman," writes Adrienne Rich in her book, *Of Woman Born*.[1] The one unifying experience shared by all men and all women is that months-long period inside a woman's body while we were formed into being. Most of us during the first years of infancy were also suckled and comforted primarily by a woman.

I am reminded of a lullaby which is not entirely soothing.

Only a poor man was Laz'rus that day.
When he lay down at the rich man's gate.
He begged for the crumbs of the rich man to eat;
He was only a tramp found dead on the street.

He was some mother's darlin';
He was some mother's son.
Once he was fair and once he was young.
Some mother rocked him, her little baby to sleep;
But they left him to die like a tramp on the street.[2]

Every person, whether pauper or prince, was at one time "some mother's darlin'." The beggar beside the street was nourished as a helpless infant by someone who at least minimally cared. Otherwise he wouldn't have made it to adulthood.

God is portrayed in Scripture in some profoundly maternal ways. The Hebrew word for God's mercy or compassion conveys the meaning of "womb-love."[3] Whenever we read about God's compassion for us, we can think of God carrying us as a mother tenderly and protectingly carries her unborn child. Womb-love is intimate and all-encompassing.

As I carried our unborn child, there was hardly a moment when I wasn't at least partially conscious of the tiny person within me. I was continually concerned that all would be well with "him." I take comfort now in knowing that God's compassion surrounds me with infinite vigilance and tenderness, much as a mother's womb encircles a fledgling fetus.

God is even described as a woman in labor: "For a long time I have kept silent, I have been quiet and held myself back. But now, like a woman in childbirth, I cry out, I gasp and pant" (Isaiah 42:14).

This strong, clear maternal image of God is reinforced by

the many images of new birth in the Bible. God birthed us into new life. We have been born again through the Spirit of a mothering God. That same ever-watching Spirit sustains us throughout our days.

While carrying our unborn baby, I was struck with how little I needed to do to shape this new being into *being*. I wrote a friend, "As the systems and limbs are invisibly knit together, we wonder in awe and await with joy the unveiling." As with Lazarus' mother, Jesus' mother, and every other mother, I simply ate, slept, and pursued my work while the most amazing processes of creation were unfolding within me! A new life that hadn't existed before would now *be* throughout all eternity. A *Newsweek* science reporter described the beginnings of human life:

> If newborns could remember and speak, they would emerge from the womb carrying tales as wondrous as Homer's. They would describe the fury of conception and the sinuous choreography of nerve cells, billions of them dancing *pas de deux* to make connections that infuse mere matter with consciousness. They would recount how the amorphous glob of an arm bud grows into the fine structure of fingers agile enough to play a polonaise. They would tell of cells swarming out of the nascent spinal cord to colonize far reaches of the embryo, helping to form face, head and glands. The explosion of such complexity and order—a heart that beats, legs that run and a brain powerful enough to contemplate its own origins—seems like a miracle.[4]

The miracle evolves without any conscious participation by the mother. Mind-boggling!

Of the hundreds of millions of sperm that begin the journey toward a waiting egg, only one manages to penetrate. Its genes merge with the egg's. That union creates a new life, though scientists don't know exactly how. The genetic code is transmitted, half from one parent and half from the other, for a new being comprising both. The code is copied from cell to cell throughout the new organism so that every cell contains "the architect's plan for the entire building." The copying takes place, incredibly, "six thousand million million million times in a human body."[5]

For me, this is humbling both in its magnitude and its microscopic complexity. I feel something akin to the childhood perplexity I had with comprehending "forever." When I began to grow dizzy and breathless, I wished there were an end sometime, somewhere. Yet contemplating "forever" led me into the mystery of God's unfathomable being. My baby's development led me toward the mystery of the Creator's infinitely intricate design.

The marvel of this creation is made even clearer by how difficult it is to imitate even just a part of it. Scientists have worked hard to create artificial limbs and organs. Understood in simplest terms, the heart is just a pump. Replacing it should be easy enough. But the human heart services 60,000 miles of blood vessels, beats 100,000 times each day, and lasts for 70 years or more.[6] As impressive as today's scientific achievements are, none matches the amazing engineering and durability of the human heart.

Embryologists have found some answers to hard questions about embryo development, but it seems as if every answer raises another question. Human hands and minds can't make a simple sea urchin. Science today is catching a glimpse of the processes that make a sea urchin—and a human. But that learning has far to go yet, and not even the most thorough explanation can minimize the wonder of the journey. A miracle described is no less a miracle!

Months ticked slowly by, and I continued to swell. This little being will not dissolve, I mused. My body cannot reverse the process and absorb these new cells back into itself. There *will* be a birth. A birth or a death. Stark alternatives. Inescapable. Inevitable. The prospect was like no other event in my life, like nothing that I had ever experienced. I was on an exhilarating, sometimes terrifying ride through life with another human being who was both a part of me and yet an independent creation.

An intimate stranger. So close and yet so unknown. Where would it all end? Never! Forever, again! My muscles, nerves, and cells in combination with those of my husband had recreated "a message to the future, carried in relays generation after generation, carried since the dim beginnings."[7] My little intimate would be another fragile link in a great chain of being that stretches through the ages.

The baby punched and kicked. The baby had rhythmic hiccups. The baby gave a startled leap when I dropped a kettle lid. An extremely jumpy person became part of my daily sensations. Was he more jumpy than he should be? I wondered. I did my best to keep the dish clatter and general hubbub to a minimum. Many a day, as the familiar hiccup pulse began, I lay down in frustration that I could do nothing to relieve it.

"Many babies hiccup in the uterus," my doctor assured me.

Very well. But can I know what is more often than usual? What symptoms signal danger? Which are part and parcel of every pregnancy? I wanted to ask more than brief sessions could answer.

My doctor acted as though it was all common knowledge, and that I shouldn't worry about a thing. He'd take care of everything. To his credit, he did explain more than other doctors I knew of in Zagreb, but he had a deft way of making me feel stupid whenever I asked an "inappropriate" question.

I'm relieved that there are experts who know more about bodies and birthing than I do. But *this* body and *this* birth were first and foremost *my* specialty. I had lived with the process every moment of every day since conception. I had intensely scrutinized every detail I could observe along the way. I wanted to play an active and intelligent part in planning the big event and in bringing it off.

Women have been told from time immemorial that childbirth is the most terrible pain endured in human life. In actuality, different women experience different levels of pain. But whether it hurts a lot or a little, delivery of a baby is a peak experience like no other, a profound mixture of anguish and joy.

Most women in history have become mothers without choice, and great numbers have lost their lives while bringing life into the world.[8] Until the last century in Western industrialized societies, and even today in numerous less-developed parts of the world, women have good reason to fear dying in childbirth. Approximately one in five labors and deliveries has some kind of complication. Until 400 years ago, most of these were fatal, either to mother or infant or both.[9]

In the 16th century the invention of obstetric forceps presented a dramatic improvement over gruesome and brutal methods in use previously.[10] Instead of hook extraction in case of failing delivery, a living child in an abnormal fetal position could now be removed from a mother without necessarily killing her in the process.

As with most technological advances, however, some supposed improvements in maternity care had very undesirable consequences. By the 17th century, the cities of Europe had an increased number of hospitals. Procedures were being developed for treatment of diseases in a more centralized fashion. Most ominous for women was the shift in maternity care: instead of a life-cycle event in the home, delivery became something of a disease. It too would henceforth be treated in hospitals, by male doctors instead of the traditional midwives.

The next two hundred years in maternity care were two hundred years of a dreadful plague which reached epidemic proportions among women hospitalized for delivery. A deadly kind of bacterial blood poisoning, named then "puerperal fever," was passed from sick patients directly to healthy mothers in delivery, on the unsterilized hands of the very physicians and surgeons into whose care they were entrusted under the new arrangement.[11] Delivery of new life brought death to untold thousands of mothers.

In the French province of Lombardy in one year not a single woman survived childbirth. A quarter of the women who gave birth in the Maternité Hospital in Paris during February 1866, died in the process.[12] We can only imagine a woman's anxiety and depression as she neared the end of her term of pregnancy facing the specter of such a death. It still takes a lot of courage to birth a baby, but we do well to recognize that the odds against us are not nearly as grim as they were a few centuries ago.

Some had suggested long ago that perhaps this puerperal fever was carried by the unwashed hands of doctors, but their concern was met with indifference and even outright hostility. The terrible truth of the cause and even prevention of the dread disease was known for decades before Lister taught the prevention of infection in surgery by asepsis and Pasteur demonstrated the reality of bacterial infection, toward the end of the 19th century. Then doctors began to wash their hands and two centuries of puerperal fever came to an end.[13] But an age of anesthetized, technologized childbirth was beginning.

Although anesthesia and other technologies aided in overcoming severe birthing difficulties, their too frequent use increasingly dehumanized the birthing process. Women were often rendered powerless by anesthesia at a time when their physical and psychic forces should have been at their peak of control and concentration.

Birthing had become anything but a normal, natural experience. Instead of being surrounded by those who could help her feel confident, relaxed, and able to cope, a woman was handled by male obstetricians who had never given birth (and never would) and who felt inclined to use all the technology at their disposal to intervene in the natural process of childbirth. In turn, women too often abdicated control over their bodies at the time of birthing, allowing "experts" to do *to* them what should rightfully be done *with* them. Radical change, however, was in the making.

In response to women's outcry (strengthened by the resurgent women's movement) maternity care began to undergo remarkable improvements. By the 1970s, childbirth practices and environments were being humanized in response to the demands of childbearing families. Obstetricians were increasingly encouraged to look to a woman's emotional needs during childbirth, in addition to her physical needs. Midwives began playing a more prominent role in providing support to women throughout labor. Mothers and fathers insisted on more active involvement in arranging the circumstances of birth. A new aura of anticipation and dynamic partnering began to surround the incomparable event of a baby's debut.

Birthing has now become a potential all-time highlight in the life of both mother and father (even if some horror stories continue). When modern medicine to the best of its ability ensures a safe delivery, and stands by supportively while mother and father labor together, the grand climax of birth can be deeply fulfilling. All participants can elatedly rejoice in the goodness of the gift of a child and the greater goodness of the Giver as they hold their little intimate, no longer stranger, in their arms for the first time.

Gerald and I experienced the goodness of the Giver, but not as we had anticipated. There was no way, the doctor declared, that Gerald could be present during labor and birth. This we had learned early in the pregnancy. Existing facilities were not adequate for privacy, he explained, and that was final! Since we wanted to identify with our Yugoslav friends, we didn't seriously consider traveling elsewhere for the delivery. I resigned myself to going it alone, attended by midwife and doctor.

I had never gleaned from my mother's stories of birthing that delivery might be a harrowing or excruciatingly painful experience. She put the emphasis on the joyful arrival of the new little person. Not all of her births were without complication and fear, but she never planted dread in my heart. Though part of me wanted to run away, I felt a great deal of confidence that I could handle the pain. After all, Mother had survived with triumph eight times and seemed only very pleased with each new child.

We waited and waited, for several weeks beyond the due

date. Will my body function properly? Do I have the resources to handle the unveiling of our intimate stranger? Will there be exhilaration or numb disappointment?

It was the Christmas season. In a letter to friends, we wrote, "Our holiday spirit is a fair mixture of hurry and wait this year. We scurry about so as not to be caught off guard, waiting all the while for the baby to break through that guard. These are in-between times."

My patience decreased in inverse proportion to my girth.

Finally on Christmas day, a normal workday in Yugoslavia, I was admitted to the hospital. With me I took *Middlemarch*, a fat novel by George Elliot, just in case nothing *really* happened. I also had the recommended paraphernalia for a self-trained Lamaze laborer. All of that equipment would prove unnecessary.

In the early stages of labor, the midwife could not find the fetal heartbeat with her fetal scope. She raised an alarm. I had been informed that she was an experienced midwife, so her panic stabbed me to the quick. I was hooked up to a fetal heart monitor which found the heartbeat but indicated fetal distress. Four more doctors rapidly converged to assess the situation. They circled around me, probing my abdomen, taking my pulse, checking the monitors, and consulting with somber tones in a language I only partially understood.

"We'll need to do a cesarean delivery," my doctor informed me. I nodded in numb resignation, fearing the worst. Who was I, to protest amid such an assembly of agitated experts? Oh, that they would just hurry to liberate my baby!

Minutes ticked by. The anesthetist was out for coffee. They would reach her soon. Are these minutes vital to my baby's life? No one reassured me.

With grim, methodical steps they prepared me for surgery. I lay powerless, a victim of forces beyond my control.
Fear dried up my emotions. Nearly paralyzed with helplessness, I must have been the picture of fortitude.

"Hang in there, stranger, babe of my love. Hold on.
They're coming to take you out."

The anesthetist finally arrived. A needle was inserted into
my arm. A strange taste filtered into my mouth, and all went
black.

2

Footloose and Fancy Free

An Illusion of Liberation

Humanity i love you
because you would rather black the boots of
success than enquire whose soul dangles from his
watch-chain which would be embarrassing for both

parties and because you
unflinchingly applaud all
songs containing the words country home and
mother when sung at the old howard

. . .

. . .   Humanity

i hate you
                              —*E. E. Cummings*[1]

I was midway through high school when the women's
liberation movement caught my imagination. A girl
friend and I stated in no uncertain terms one day that
we intended to be career women and that we would not be

marrying. It was bold fun to set ourselves off from the pack. Which career I would eventually choose was beside the point. The prospect of a future unlimited by traditional prejudices and stereotypes was a heady potion for an ambitious young woman. Exhilarated by promises of liberation *to be and do whatever one desired,* I resolved to prove my self-determination in not being victimized by tradition.

What did it really mean to be "for women's lib?" I could not have spelled it out in much detail. Instinctively I knew my allegiance was with it. I didn't belong to the movement in any organized way, but it belonged to me. Mine was a vague, private identification with its cause as I understood it, a cause which claimed that women were unfairly put down, boxed in, and discriminated against on the job, at home, and at church.

Early on in my acquaintance with the movement, its *symbols* of liberation spoke louder to me than the *substance* of the movement. Take the bra-burning, for example. Its alleged occurrence was relevant to me and my high school peers.

The high school we attended was private and religious. In the late 1960s it required girls to wear distinctive clothing. Not only were dress lengths regulated, but we were asked to construct our dresses with two thicknesses of fabric above the waist. The outer layer was called a "cape." All this in the era of the miniskirt made us a quaint spectacle. Thus bedecked, we were quite amused with the idea of bra-burning and found it loaded with significance. We threatened to imitate with a bonfire of dress capes on the school's front lawn at graduation.

I value my religious heritage for instilling an appreciation of natural beauty and simplicity in dress. But young women like me were caught in a bind between two standards. The religious subculture made almost a fetish of modesty in dress codes; the "world" around us indulged in exploitive exhibition of female sexuality. One message urged us to cover up lest we provoke the males among us. The other suggested we cultivate cute, sexy charms to attract the males. In both cases, our female sexuality was an object, whether of fear or exploitation.

The women's movement offered a corrective. I embraced its critique of stereotypically feminine, restrictive clothing. Whose insanity is it when women wobble on spindly heels, sleep on huge hair rollers, squeeze into panty girdles that chafe, and walk through bad weather in sheer stockings and flimsy skirts? Why did we grow up aching for our first nylon stockings, our first eye makeup, our first pair of heels, our first expensive perfume?

In the gym locker room I discovered how much status could be conferred on the girls who paraded in bras and girdles (whether they needed them or not). Would the womanhood they betokened be just as empty? Imagery and wiles, the symbols of a gimmicky femininity, could not show the way to compassion and character.

It was invigorating to know I could resist the cultural expectation that women be irrational, mindless, and interested only in trivia of personal appearance. The old advice, "Girls, be witty if you must; be pretty if you can; but be sweet if it kills you!" could now be discarded out of hand. No sweethearting for me! I retorted. The classy lady crowned with an expensive coiffure and painted with makeup on *Cosmopolitan's* cover would no longer dictate acceptability for me. Plain and natural me was just fine!

Feminists held up a new way, a way in which academic

study and a career were lauded as the qualifications that determined the value of a woman. I loved the discipline of study and writing and savored academic rewards. Ideas and good discussions were "the staff of life," far more enriching than superficial small talk and giddy parties.

After high school I pushed on to college, eager to cut my teeth on new ideas. Before long I heard a curious expression bandied about in the dorm: "match factory." College a match factory? It was news to me that women *actually* went to college primarily to find a mate. Chalk it up to the naivete of my idealism. I was serious about education. To do it even for its money or prestige value seemed to me an adulteration of the pure pursuit of wisdom and knowledge.

It wasn't that I was averse to friendships with men. But when one special friend pressured me to "go steady" I told my journal, "I'm not ready to give up my independence, doing my own thing. He said he thought that was kind of selfish, but I don't! I don't want to be smothered by one other person's attention, affection, and ideas. Sure, I'm not independent of people—but I'd rather keep the spectrum wide."

Never was it my primary goal to find a husband, or even a "steady." Thanks to my parents and to the women's movement, I knew I didn't need to be attached to a man to be a worthwhile person.

Others could play at dating games in the dim lounges of the dorm and under leafy arbors on "the hill." I preferred authentic relationships. The whole dating charade was undergoing metamorphosis in the culture at large. My friends and I grasped for new vocabulary, for new definitions.

"Well, what *do* you call a male-female relationship, if not 'dating'?" my sister challenged me one evening.

"How about, 'friendship based on mutual appreciation of personhood'?" Quite a mouthful—cumbersome and unwieldy, but closer perhaps to the essence. Ah, the essence of things!

An acquaintance shocked me one day by saying, "I'm afraid I'll have to go into full-time Christian service if I don't get married." I could scarcely believe my ears. To imagine that marriage was an alternative to the responsibility of daily discipleship was ludicrous. I was often tempted to disdain those who were simply biding their time until Prince Charming would relieve them of the need to choose their own destiny.

Another acquaintance, eager with waiting, said her beau had hinted that he might be getting her a ring, but that he hadn't decided for sure. Was she merely a pawn? I wondered. Why did she allow herself to be the passive recipient of such a momentous decision? When another friend openly admitted to a need for marriage and close companionship, I was amazed again. In a way I admired her honesty. What was it though, that left her feeling incapable of pursuing her own unique calling?

Many women in my mother's generation had heeded primarily the call to get married and have children. Motherhood for a married woman was taken for granted, since contraceptive practices were less extensive then. Women often included maternity dresses as part of their trousseau. Oh yes, there were some gifted women who gave themselves to exceptional services outside of family settings, but the choice not to marry, and not to have children if married, was rare indeed.

Ours was a new generation, filled with new opportunities. We had examined and disposed of the "motherhood myth."

At least some of my peers felt sure that neither pregnancy nor motherhood would be the most fulfilling experience in our lives. We saw parenting as an unacceptable drag on ambition and an interference to self-development.

Feminist Robin Morgan wrote in 1970: "One thing does seem clearer as time goes on: the nuclear family unit is oppressive to women (*and* children, *and* men). The woman is forced into a totally dependent position, paying for her keep with an enormous amount of emotional and physical labor which is not even considered work.... In essence, women are still back in feudal times."[2]

Liberation, the more militant of feminists argued, means liberation from being stuck with primary care of demanding little dependents. Caring for children, they claimed, saps the energies, dulls the mind, and ruins the love life. Child care was considered to be so circumscribing and demeaning that any competent person would surely choose another line of work. Some urged that child care centers be made mandatory in society, to *free* women from children. Freedom and children were seen as antithetical.

The ensnarement of an "everyday housewife" became proverbial. Any woman who allowed herself to fall into the traditional marriage and motherhood trap courted scorn from "enlightened" persons like myself. After all, anyone by virtue of biology alone can become a mother or father, I thought. Competence has little to do with it. Who in the world, with any wits about her, would allow herself to become victim to 24-hour vigils, rowdy interrupting kids, and tubs of laundry and dishes?

I found women with little children singularly uninteresting. Women who appeared unable to control their lives effectively hardly served as attractive role models. I especially pitied pregnant women with their clumsy gait and puffy faces, secretly blaming them for their own undesirable girth.

In addition, it was hard to feel any real affection for the resultant obstreperous little ogres who loudly demanded to control the serious conversations I longed to have with former friends whose misfortune it now was to be their parents.

And then I turned my critical gaze upon my parents. Rather than recognizing that they had taught me much of my resistance to passive, pampered femininity, I turned accuser.

"Mother, how could you let it happen to you? Why have eight children? Why stay home to maintain this ungrateful bunch? Imagine all you could have done if you hadn't enslaved yourself to your family!" (This—to the one who had sustained my very existence!)

"And Dad, why don't you ever wash dishes or clean the house? Why do you assume that your job has priority over Mother's involvements?" To younger brothers listening in, I had become a "radical sis."

Mother and Dad, only slightly fazed by my onslaught, emphasized their joy with family life and their deep satisfaction with their lifestyle. Surely they were fooling themselves, I mused.

Our generation has frequently and unflatteringly been called the "me generation" or the "narcissistic generation." What is generally meant, I think, is that we have been enamored with ourselves and our self-fulfillment at the expense of service to our world.

Was the women's movement part of the problem or part of the solution? Many persons simplistically wrote off all feminists as obnoxious, egotistic women. They held that the women's movement was fanning the flames of a woman's base selfishness, bringing in a generation of women who lust after the limelight and neglect their families.

"Self-development is a higher duty than self-sacrifice," in the words of an early feminist. Did such statements license every woman to do her own thing in her own way?

I grew increasingly uneasy with feminists who were portrayed as hostile and anti-male. I was also uncomfortable with some of their tactics. I didn't really consider men in general to be oppressors and class enemies. Yet I still wanted to listen and probe deeper to understand what feeds the hostility between the sexes.

The women's movement resurgence arose largely among women who had been active in the civil rights movement, in the antiwar movement, in student movements, and in the political left. There is something remarkably contagious about demanding freedom. Especially among women, who make up the oldest oppressed group on the face of the planet, did the door to freedom appear powerfully attractive. I, too, was attracted, yet dragged my feet. Something was amiss.

Books like *The First Sex* advocated female supremacy, appealing to ranks of women who had caught the heady scent of power available to those on top. A radio talk show guest argued that "in order for women to be fully liberated, they'll need to depend on a new servant class." A newspaper column suggested further that what most employed women now need is a *"wife"* to run their errands, take their kids to school, clean the stove, and prepare dinner.

Where was the integrity of a liberation that was forced to create a new class of (oppressed) servants just to shore up a class of powerful new exploiters (now in female garb)?

I began to feel that feminists might have overrated the masculine values of competition and success, while properly seeking to correct injustice toward women. Taking on the manner of our oppressors was surely not the solution.

Up until this point, my engagement with the issues raised by the women's movement was not very profound. Perhaps I would have been less hopeful of an adequate resolution of these tensions in my response to those issues if I had not begun to discover yet another perspective that helped me get beyond that dialogue of caricatures. I found the work of biblical feminists taking up some of the new wine without losing all of the ancient wisdom.

Biblical feminists offered the insight that affirms the oneness of men and women in Christ, and our freedom to serve one another in radically new ways. They pointed out that wanting to win in the job market and achieving full liberation are two very different goals in the women's movement. To win, women and men must play the same game by the established rules, conforming to existing structures. The winner pushes ahead of the others to get to the top, "lording it over" in the same oppressive ways that have gone on for centuries.

To be free, in contrast, means that men and women can give up power or use power to *change the game*. Liberated persons are free to enhance others while deriving more satisfaction from the service rendered than from its payoff in wages or prestige.

I will always feel indebted to brave, outspoken women for challenging me and thousands of other women to enlarge our horizons and remove the bushel basket that was concealing the light we had to share. I credit the women's movement for cracking open a narrow box of traditional female jobs and giving women choices to branch out. Women have begun to give of themselves in ways they had only rarely found accessible before.

When I set out to succeed in academics, I did so believing that self-sufficiency and intellectual prowess were marks of the liberated woman. The angry early rhetoric of the women's movement did shape my view that motherhood was not an appropriate choice for a woman who hoped to be liberated.

Even so, when I was midway through college, some relevant thoughts from Thomas Merton found their way into my journal. They reflect a twinge of conscience that kept me from being entirely swept away by arrogance:

> She who isolates herself in order to enjoy a kind of independence in her egotistic and external self does not find unity at all.... There is no true peace possible for the woman who still imagines that some accident of talent or grace or virtue segregates her from other women and places her above them.... God does not give us graces or talents or virtues for ourselves alone. We are members one of another and everything that is given to one member is given for the whole body.[3] (*I have feminized the pronouns.*)

What I didn't fully understand in my youngest adult years was that ambition and success do not add up to liberation. Striving for excellence to prove oneself superior is only an illusion of liberation. Striving to serve others more excellently—this is liberation far more profound!

3

The Hidden Program

Joys of Family Life

My dear children.... You must know that there is nothing higher and stronger and more wholesome and good for life in the future than some good memory, especially a memory of childhood, of home. People talk to you a great deal about your education, but *some good sacred memory, preserved from childhood, is perhaps the best education.* If a man carries many such memories with him into life, he is safe to the end of his days. And if one has only one good memory left in one's heart, even that may sometime be the *means of saving him.*

—Alyosha, in *Brothers Karamazov*[1]

A feature article not long ago in our Chicago paper told of an old man named George, who died on the first day of the New Year. George's hospital bed chart read: "No family, no friends." All the adventures and all the heartbreak George experienced in his 79 years of life, he kept to himself. He used to spend his mornings sitting in the district police station, resting his feet, and watching events. After he left the station, he rode the buses all day.

Eventually George was noticed there in the police station, and one of the officers invited George to his home for Christmas Day. George found a chair, sat down, and watched it all. The children had a present for him, too. When the officer asked him if he had children of his own, George began to cry.

On his way home, George asked if he could do what he wished with the gift. He was told he could. So George wrapped it up again, tied the ribbons, and gave it to the man at the diner who sometimes served him a free meal. Just about everything that people gave to George, he turned around and shared with somebody else.

George died on New Year's Day. There were no flowers, no wake, no funeral, no graveside services. Only two mourners (from the police station) showed up at the cemetery to pay their respects.

"George White died simple," the article concludes. "He could have died forgotten, which happens often in this city to old people like George. But he wasn't."[2]

While I read this account, Joan Baez's mellow "Amazing Grace" came over the radio waves. Something snapped deep within me and the tears poured forth. I readily admit to an abundant share of sentiment, but this outburst came from far below the surface. Buried in the core of my being was the awareness that familial love is what truly matters to me, an amazing grace throughout my life. The grace from above is most profoundly made tangible in our families at home and among the family of God.

The tragedy of a lonely man dying without family or friends strikes at the root of that which makes us essentially human—*being in relationship*. George's dignity despite his loneliness demonstrates the tenacity of the human spirit and the capacity to be gracious even in grief and aloneness.

The role of father, mother, and children is "the absolutely critical center of social force," writes social critic Michael Novak. Even when poverty and tragedy strike, as they so often do, it is the family who defends individuals against alienation and despair. Through all the injustices and disasters of the last thousand years, one unforgettable law has been learned: if things go well with the family, life is worth living; when the family falters, life falls apart.[3]

The family nourishes "basic trust" within children. From this trust spring creativity, psychic energy, social vitality. If the quality of family life disintegrates, there is no "quality of life."[4] If we cease to love and enjoy children, the human race will have no future, no little ones to nourish and teach, no community, no wisdom, no grace.

There may be two kinds of people in this world, Novak notes further: "individual people" and "family people."[5] Our society, for the most part, celebrates the former and denigrates the latter. Success in public life is held quite separate from success in the home. Highly paid, mobile professionals may disdain the family and its obligations while rarely stopping to acknowledge that they have been nurtured by its strengths.

As a young college student I was more inclined to condemn the traditions than to admit that I was privileged because of my own family roots. But even while my separate self, proud and cynical, was ruling my conscious choices, a subterranean stream of love and loyalty ran deep within me. The stream surfaced occasionally to rejuvenate my joy in the bonds of affection and trust that made our family work.

Consciously I strove to be a liberated and self-sufficient individual. Unconsciously I never relinquished the vision of wholehearted robust family life as the ideal setting for the development of my full humanity.

Families vary widely, of course. Yet no matter how old we are, or how early we left home, many of us feel in our own unique way a profound, primal bond with our parents. They knew us during our dimly remembered beginnings—a time few other people ever glimpsed. When the days of our childhood are over and the people who signified the goodness and pain of those days are gone, part of us is gone.

Home has been described in ideal terms as "a safe place . . . a fortress where its members are free from attack. Though each is different, the personhood of each is affirmed."[6] (We are being forced to recognize today how few of the homes in our society actually fit this description.)

I was only six years old when I ventured forth from home, with my siblings, to attend a boarding school for weeks at a time. My folks were church workers in Ethiopia then. Mother and Dad made the most of our weekends and vacation time at home, planning numerous special excursions and fun times for the family. The bumpy return from school in a pickup truck was smoothed by the knowledge that Mother and Dad were eager for our arrival; they took obvious pleasure in our presence.

My parents strenuously disagreed with a philosophy of church work then popular, that put church tasks ahead of family concerns, especially for missionaries. In their approach, ministry and family life were thoroughly integrated. They considered their family to be a witness in and of itself. (With the eight of us creating sundry crises, I imagine this was clearer at some times than others!) *But what better way to teach redemptive relationships than to model them in a family?* Boarding school was a reluctant compromise, not a means for removing the children so the parents could get on with "real work."

Dad was introduced not long ago in a public gathering as a man who "knows how to be a father." He has worked at many things: teaching, growing grapes, administering a school, preaching, and more. But the profession closest to his heart is that of husband and father.

When I told Dad recently that children have begun to win my heart, his immediate response was, "Now you're learning. *Now* you're learning! We had eight because we just enjoyed them *so much.*"

I didn't hear Dad telling me I could only find fulfillment in having children. I know better. He's talking from his heart about the delight he has experienced within a family circle and wanting that same joy for his children.

I marvel at Mother. I don't recall hearing her complain about all the work her eight offspring brought her. She was nobody's doormat. Nor was she so entirely selfless as to be left limp and washed out by it all. To the contrary, she exudes energy today and amazes us with her myriad activities. But I will never comprehend how she maintained her dignity while diapering and toilet-training eight. What kept her sane through untold numbers of interrupted nights, multitudinous childhood diseases (even tropical varieties), many transatlantic travels, and enough spilled milk to make anyone cry?

I have a sneaking suspicion that the way Dad enjoyed fathering made mothering bearable, if not always fun. (The sharing of burdens strongly hints at the mutuality which I deem essential to authentic liberation.)

Mother's concern throughout was not how nice a house she could keep, or how fancy her entertainment could be. More important to her was that each of her children be loved, listened to, and affirmed. In Mother we knew we always had an advocate. Instead of lavish gifts or elaborate parties, she gave herself. The hours we spent at her knee as she read to us were among the high points of our childhood.

Like most other folks, my recollections of childhood are a mixture of pleasure and pain, nostalgia and some regret. I cannot undo or redo my past. My family has played a decisive role in shaping my particular strengths *and* weaknesses. I can blame it for my faults or praise it for giving me life and love. My family, despite its imperfections, has been a crucible where faith and repentance bring redemption. I hope to pass on to my children all that was generous, loving, peaceful, and pure, thus becoming a strong link in the chain of generations.

One of the most persuasive arguments in favor of family life is the mutual support the members can give one another. It is often true that no other relationships are as sturdy and meaningful. There come times in each of our lives—news of cancer, death of a child, severe misfortune—when nothing else matters except having family and friends with whom to weep and embrace!

In our current society there are powerful forces pulling our families in different directions. On the one side, our capitalist system demands hard work, sober cooperation, and sacrifice. On the other, it stresses competition and independence, encouraging hedonism and consumption. Persons who have most internalized the values of capitalism are rendered most liable to the enormous centrifugal forces that shear marriages and families apart.[7]

The spirit of materialistic consumption diminishes our concern for the well-being of the whole community, and for families in particular. Countless families have been virtually fatherless, and now motherless as well, because of the value we place on the paunchy paycheck and all the gadgets it buys. The *worst pressures of all* hit the families without jobs and without income in this society of spenders.

Most Americans would claim that our system puts family concerns high on the agenda. Rousing presidential pep talks laud the virtues of the traditional family. Bedrock familial values, however, are continually undermined by the same system—a system which so often puts profits before people; a system that glorifies violence, lusts for material gain, crushes those who are weak, and scorns those who fail to accomplish the American dream for themselves.

Some antiestablishment factions in our society also have a negative impact on families. The liberal intelligentsia has taught that the traditional family is a problem, and seeks to liberate people from it. They see families putting an inhibiting constraint on individual freedoms.

The sharpened tones of debate over pros and cons of the traditional patriarchal family have greatly politicized the choices which every woman faces. If she chooses a career instead of family she is labeled anti-family. If she chooses to marry and raise children she appears to reject liberation.

But many of us are not comfortable with such sharp polarization between careers or children, freedom or family. In recent years some persons at both ends of the spectrum have tried to take the goals of the other into account, attempting to resolve the tension in more acceptable ways.

Today's families are caught midstream in some turbulent transitions. Many people warn that the traditional nuclear family is in serious decline. But in spite of the doomsayers, I see reason for hope. When basic assumptions are challenged, new courses can be charted, using the best from what tradition offers and discarding the worst. Times of transition are filled with vulnerability and chaos, yes, but also opportunities to renew our commitment to the true family ideal.

Why are families changing? Sociologist John Scanzoni notes the concern for women's individual rights and well-being at the expense of maintaining families as a traditional institution. Traditional family structures have prohibited most women from moving into meaningful *work* experiences outside their homes. Their responsibilities were generally limited to the home front.

Those same family structures, Scanzoni observes, have prevented men from enjoying meaningful love experiences. They have been too busy making money to participate fully in nurturing family experiences.

It isn't easy to balance the well-being of the familial institution with the well-being of the individuals that make it up. Scanzoni appropriates from Freud the insight that adults need more than anything else to *work* and to *love*. The ideal family, Scanzoni suggests, provides maximum opportunities for all its members to *love* and to *work*. He hails present trends toward new traditions that balance the work of individuals with care for the well-being of the family unit. Families who achieve this for all their members will move beyond the limits of traditional bonds and individualism alike.[8] Isaiah 11, one of the Bible's most powerful pictures of hope, describes a fresh green shoot bravely raising its head to the sky from a broken, decaying stump. I am excited to think that from the rubble of the present transitions in our society we can yet find *a way* to bring home good news for our families. Those of us who walk in this way cherish our children above all because they show us the way to the kingdom. Along this way, we respect our women as staunch disciples who tenderly mother their young and courageously proclaim the good news in all walks of life. On this way we love our men who devotedly give themselves to their wives and children as Christ gave himself to the church, and who serve a broken world with gentle strength. We also esteem our single men and women for the special responsibilities they alone can shoulder in the family of God. By finding better ways to include child-free persons in families with us, we can only be strengthened.

Weak knees, be strong! Indecisive wills, be resolute! Wavering loyalties, be firm! It is up to all of us, *men and women*, to nurture our families lest what we most treasure be splintered into oblivion, or stratified into oppressive hierarchies. Would that the tender sprout of our families— nurtured with love, mutual respect, and fairness—will grow and flourish and bear abundant fruit. A heritage of good childhood memories will carry our children safely to the end of their days.

4

A Season Out of Sync

Marital Adjustment

I love you. Please don't let that stand in the way of our friendship.

—*Ray Fitzgerald*

I remember after getting your first phone call, beating my fists against the wall, yelling, "Oh no! Oh no!" Quite insane perhaps, but somehow I was afraid that here again, like often before, I'd have to be nice but gradually work through and refuse someone else's affection. It just overwhelmed me.

—*My journal, 1974*

In the fall of my junior year at college I participated in an ad hoc group of six or seven juniors and seniors who met regularly for discussion and recreation. We had no guiding motive other than free-for-all interaction on a regular basis. Our first gathering was slated as a discussion of Ralph Waldo Emerson's essay on self-reliance.

Gerald Shenk was instrumental in forming the group. In

the context of the group's animated discussions friendship budded between Gerald and me. But when he invited me one evening to join him in watching the launch of a homemade hot-air balloon across the valley, I was taken by surprise. I was uncomfortable with being singled out of the group. Romantic attachments were almost taboo in the group (although an unspoken taboo).

Despite my reservations it wasn't many weeks before I confided to my journal: "Gerald, it's finally struck me right between the eyes—the beginning of love and a willingness to invest myself in a relationship. My mind is blown, my reason eclipsed, my whole rational balance upset. I'm a mad woman, seeing with bleary eyes, entirely out of control. Gerald, I'm a new person. I've been transformed. I never knew it could be like this."

There's some realism in Scott Peck's view that romance is "a trick that our genes pull on our otherwise perceptive mind to hoodwink or trap us into marriage." He further suggests in *The Road Less Traveled* that a function of falling in love is "to provide the participants with a magic cloak of omnipotence which blissfully blinds them to the riskiness of what they are doing when they undertake marriage."[1]

Some astonishing changes were noted in my journal after several months of more frequent but circumspect encounters with Gerald:

> My battles for independence, freedom from myself, my family, and background are no longer important. He's cracked the image that many have of me and allowed the little spirit that's been rattling around in the larger hollow image to express itself. Gerald is the epitome of a free person, and to be with him is to be free. More free, I think, than I've ever felt before. I'll have to write poetry. This

journalistic scrawl is inadequate in expressing the joy of being together.

Hoodwinked? In part, yes. And I did recover from the
craze to bring things back into focus. Some ambivalence appears in an entry a bit later:

> I fear what an exclusive one-to-one relationship will do to
> my larger circle of friends. Will we be ostracized if we spend
> a lot of time together? My independence is very precious to
> me. This becomes more and more obvious when I sense that
> it might be decreasing, or that it might be taken away from
> me. The prospects are more exciting, but I don't want it to
> make me more incapable of managing alone.

And then I left campus for three months of study in
Europe. Gerald wondered what would become of our relationship. Again, my journal was the recipient of my musings,
more tempered than earlier. "If we come together again," I
wrote, "and it seems right, fine; but in my future planning,
the continuance of this relationship is not essential. I still
have my own life to live independent of anyone, that is in
response to God's call. If God brings us together again, I will
rejoice. If not, I'll look for something better."

In a large measure it was Gerald's fair play that eased my
fears about independence and dependence. An excerpt from
one of his voluminous letters to Europe in the next phase of
our relationship illustrates my point.

> Sara, when I try to understand my feelings about you I
> realize that I feel fiercely gentle; lovingly protective yet
> wanting to see you struggle for yourself; wanting you to be
> loyal and committed to me yet wanting you to be strong and
> independent; wanting you to be able to be submissive
> (wanting to be worthy of that submission) yet wanting you

to be free, a whole person in your own right; wishing so much to be with you yet wanting to be able to stand apart.

I like the description of education as the process whereby one changes from a cocky know-it-all attitude to a state of considered, thoughtful ignorance. Learning commitment and love as we moved toward partnership was that sort of education for us. I began to dream. I had caught a glimpse of a love I had not allowed myself to believe possible, and so thinking, had never expected it or accepted it from anyone else.

Life shared with an intimate friend can be much fuller than life spent alone, I concluded, provided it doesn't include a possessiveness that limits contact with other friends. I had some misgivings about the work, time, and commitment necessary to nurture a relationship. Even so, I wrote to Gerald:

> I don't want to settle for less than the best; believe me, if it takes work, I mean to work at this! My earlier reluctance hinged on my uncertainty that the potential for the kind of relationship I've envisioned exists, but as I am more and more affirmed in that, I see all kinds of exciting possibilities. Oh, and faith is such an essential element.

Throughout our senior year of college Gerald and I spent many fine hours together: editing and writing for the college paper, creating a radio feature program, hiking, biking, and yes, even studying on occasion. Our plans for the future converged and came clear. We both wanted to pursue further training in theology. A fellowship program for first-year expenses at the seminary or divinity school of one's choice made this option feasible for us. (We were both finalists in the competition; they eventually gave the award to Gerald, but we used it together!)

On a beautiful sunlit morning in early July we sealed our marriage covenant before friends and families gathered under a huge elm in my folks' backyard. I told Gerald on that occasion:

> When this all began between us I wasn't very hopeful. With single-mindedness I was preparing to go it alone. Gerald, your warmth and willingness to give of yourself melted my tower of resistance. To love you is to dare to give up myself as the center of meaning and to give my life to God's transcendent plan for our life together.

"And finally," we vowed to each other, "we give ourselves as full partners for life, in service to each other in our home and to others in our world."

Then we were off for seminary in California, riding high on a wave of great expectations. That same wave (fickle as waves are wont to be) abruptly sucked us under and twisted us over and over before throwing us up on the shore.

Marriage defeated me. I relinquished my demands on myself to achieve; I slipped into a more passive, supportive role. Although I had raised my consciousness about who I as a woman could be, the childish expectation was deeply ingrained within me that my prince would carry me off to his castle in the clouds. Suddenly, I wanted nothing more than to be his helpless princess. I worked hard at my seminary studies, but I wanted my husband to be five steps ahead of me. Wasn't he supposed to be the leader?

Why couldn't I receive my sense of importance and social identity through my husband's involvements, like many other women did? Intellectually I knew that vicarious identification was a strange way to find relevance in life. But secretly I envied women who could revel in fame and fortune because their husbands were stars.

This gutsy, hardheaded woman suddenly wanted it all on a silver platter. I told Gerald, "Let me ride on your coattails! I really prefer to be a private, supportive kind of person." I secretly expected Gerald to be wise enough to make the decisions and strong enough to launch us *both* on a brilliant career.

For all of Gerald's fine qualities and potential, instant maturity and success were not his to offer. By trying to hide behind my husband, I placed a cruel and impossible burden on him to achieve for both of us. He had bargained for a partnership; I wanted a knight. More fundamentally, I was reneging on my responsibility before God to develop and use the gifts with which God had endowed *me*.

Gerald and I have not had a static relationship. If things aren't getting better, they are getting worse. I had thought I knew what it takes to make a marriage work. That was, of course, in my flushed elation before marriage. I had walked into a complex, adult relationship with the simplemindedness of a child!

What is more foolish or profound than marriage? Two persons promise to share life together on all levels—physical, economic, spiritual. This promise is made in the face of certain change, upheaval, and death. It is no surprise that one or both of its partners buckle under the strain and flounder in doubt and uncertainty.

Couples today face the issues of women's and men's roles in a way that earlier generations rarely did. Struggles of dominance and submission, of personal identity in relation to spouse, of commitment to service and personal calling before God are all factors that can bring much stress into a marriage. They can lead to unity and vision, or to disunity and loss of perspective. The couple's level of commitment to each other determines which path they follow. Faithfulness to God, each other, and to a community of faith are essential tools in the struggle.

Mark Twain observed that no couple could begin to know the bliss of being married short of 25 years together. It used to be considered radical to seek divorce. Now it seems radical to stay married, especially for 25 years.

We labored our way through storm after storm during our first years. In our favor was an enduring affection and a profound mutual respect that permitted honest searching and frank analysis. Against us was the baggage of patriarchy which kept surfacing in my conscious expectations. It seemed that the world and the church had contrived to make me *need* to idolize my husband. Intellectually I argued in favor of partnership. Emotionally, however, I found myself succumbing to cultural conditioning. A power beyond my control kept dragging me back, submerging me in a wistful desire that my husband cover for all my shortcomings and insecurities.

Gerald, to his enduring credit, consistently and adamantly refused to allow me to slip behind. It takes a sensitive, secure man to urge that his wife equal or better his achievement. Gerald applauded my achievement whenever I was honored for some academic success.

On one occasion Gerald wrote to me, imaging our partnership within a colossal orchestra:

> In some of the orchestra's themes we will only have bit parts, in others we may have duets; eventually you will have an

important solo in a major work and I will be right there to
support and uphold. In another I may have a solo, and yet I
will know you are with me. We can make music!

As time proceeded, I began to see that I was making us
both losers by reining myself back in the hope of enhancing
Gerald's image.

"I have a change of heart," I recorded one day in my
journal. "The hound of heaven pursued me all year. Finally
I have decided to give full diligence in my own pursuit of
seminary studies. I've made excuses all year, seeking to
remain irresponsible. I was psychologically conditioned to
expect my husband to create a future for me. Yet somehow
the Spirit will not let me go."

"Lord," I prayed, "enliven and quicken my mind.
Radically reorient my motivation. You refuse to allow me to
sink into Gerald's shadow. It is exciting to think that you
want to use my mind. I feel like a newborn, eager child today. Thank you for the rebirth."

Growing within me was the conviction that commitment
to God means an obligation to use my abilities to honor their
Creator. It is wrong and sinful to hide behind my husband's
(or children's) identities. My husband is not my salvation.
He is my partner, and my friend. He is *not* my savior or my
lord. His sturdy love buoys me up when I'm down. I derive
joy from his activities and his successes. But these belong to
him. They don't cover for us both. His involvements must
not swallow up my gifts, my calling, or my responsibility to
minister to others. My own calling is unique; bound up with
his calling in some ways, yet also uniquely my own, a
response to God's design for *my* life. I choose deliberately to
embrace it.

Dorothy van Woerkom has adapted from a German folk-tale the marvelous story called *The Queen Who Couldn't Bake Gingerbread.*[2] King Pilaf wanted to marry, but only under certain conditions. His queen must be wise and beautiful. She must also bake perfect gingerbread. However, through a lengthy set of diplomatic negotiations, he finally settled on a princess who could not bake gingerbread.

She, in turn, had her own demand. Her king must play the slide trombone. It took even more diplomacy for them both to agree to set their particular conditions aside. Neither would mention "gingerbread" or "slide trombone" again. But, of course, one day they did. This led to a spat, a grouchy retreat to opposite ends of the castle, and grudges nursed for days.

The genius of the tale is its not-so-fairy-tale resolution of the conflict. The odors of baking practice came from one end of the castle; the beginnings of music practice came from the other. The scene was set for reconciliation.

Lo and behold! The king brought the gingerbread; the queen delivered a melody on the slide trombone. Harmony prevailed when they each dropped their preconceived notions of what their mate should be like, and changed themselves instead.

A delicate balancing act is central to every marriage. Flexibility rather than role rigidity makes balance and harmony more possible.

Dance is the metaphor I find most apt in describing marriage. A man and woman in intimate relationship are continually in motion: teaching, learning, forgiving, and being forgiven. Sometimes the husband provides refuge and strength for his wife; sometimes he feels hurt and helpless and wants to lean on her for comfort. Each spouse is on occasion a child, a parent, a lover, a sister, a brother, a follower, a leader. Day in and day out, the dance goes on.

The fellowship of husband and wife reflects the dynamic mutuality and reciprocity of the Trinity, who agreed, "Let us make man in our image." (The clear sense of the text here is "man" as male and female.) The highest type of companionship is possible in a marriage where the worth and dignity of each partner are recognized. Men and women alike participate in the divine image, but their *fellowship* as male and female is the essence of what it *means* to be in the image of God, as Paul Jewett has ably argued.[3] In the order of creation, man and woman are properly related when they accept each other as *equals* whose differences are mutually complementary in all spheres of life and human endeavor.[4] Man and woman are not to be competitors, nor lords and slaves, but full partners in family life and in fulfilling God's will on earth.

God created us not in isolation, but in relationship. It is in personal relationship that humans (male and female) become persons in God's image. "Person" is man and woman together, an indissoluble complementarity.[5] (This complementarity refers not only to the marriage bond, but to general cooperation of males and females.)

Together man and woman are to build the world, but not the macho world of an endless race for power, nor a civilization which asserts the priority of things over persons. Building the world together necessitates that women throw off an unhealthy dependency and passivity and that men resist the temptation to pull rank. Women and men must awaken to the *supreme value* of successful, stable, and profound relationships, for in so doing they aspire most nearly to embodying the image of God.

What is all the talk about the headship of the husband, and the wife's obligation to submit? Is not some hierarchy of leaders and followers, of more responsible and less responsible, desirable? Isn't the biblical model more like a ladder with steps that indicate each person's respective position, than a dance of equal partners?

What I find striking in this regard is that every time Paul calls for submission by a group of people, the reason is *never* because of one's rung on the hierarchy. The reason one submits is because Jesus lived a life of submission. Each of us, husband or wife, is asked to imitate Jesus, who though he was rich, became poor; though he was God, became a servant; though he had power, gave it up in the face of death.[6]

"Be imitators of God, therefore, as dearly loved children," the apostle Paul writes, "and live a life of love, just as Christ loved us and gave himself up for us as a fragrant offering and sacrifice to God" (Ephesians 5:1, 2).

Further on (in Ephesians 5:22-23) wives are enjoined to submit to their husbands, and husbands are commanded to love their wives. Is there a big distinction? A difference between submitting and loving is not supported either by the teachings of Jesus or by Paul's own context in Ephesians 5.[7] A husband's love is a love that involves a husband's submission. The model of love is the self-emptying of Christ which Paul described in Philippians 2:3-8. The Christlike husband takes upon himself the form of a servant, humbles himself, and dies to himself by living for the best interests of his family.

Does such a submissive love turn a husband into a passive, henpecked pushover? Not in the least! Too often we think that if we don't treat our husbands as kings and defer to their every whim they will either kick us out or collapse from neglect. What we forget is that the key to true and just authority is servanthood. Aggressive, dynamic servanthood does not make a doormat of anyone. Within the aura of such authority each member of the family can flourish and willingly submit to the good of all. Authority doesn't imply privilege and status, but rather the power to *give* of oneself for the other's well-being. Submission does not mean passivity, but rather a chosen, willing self-giving which engenders joyful participation by all.

But, some will ask, doesn't headship mean being in charge? "Head" as used metaphorically in the New Testament points overwhelmingly *not* to a corporate organizational chart, but to a dynamic, organic, living unity.[8] Christ is "the Head, from whom the whole body, supported and held together by its ligaments and sinews, grows as God causes it to grow" (Colossians 2:19). The "head" of this living organism is not its ruler but the source of its life. What the "head" is in charge of, on this reading, is *serving* the other members in his family.

Marriage as a dance of two free, respecting, and mutually submissive persons transcends the kind of cooperation stressed in purely egalitarian, contractually based marriages. Mutual servanthood in marriage isn't a model which encourages two individuals merely to live together while remaining detached and uninvolved in each other's lives. The contemporary women's movement fosters this on occasion, as the ideal of true liberation. A marriage contracted to ensure complete egalitarianism falls short of the biblical idea.

Mutual servanthood is a product of grace, the response and responsibility of all Christians in marriage. Serving one another in love is not slavery because it is always voluntary. I choose to serve the one I love. I am not his slave. He chooses to serve me. He is not my boss. My husband respects me equally as much as I respect him. He respects my ministry. I respect his.

It was in meeting someone who shared my vision that I considered marriage in the first place. Moving from independence to interdependence was much more complex and entangling than I anticipated. Yet through the years our bond of affection had become more liberating and nourishing than in the beginning when it was nearly ripped apart. By doing all in our power to sustain our commitment we found our love so increased as to become a haven of rest and an avenue to true freedom.

Enormous changes loomed just ahead. What would a baby's birth do to our strong and yet ever vulnerable union? Might it start a chain reaction of events that would limit my horizons? Would we fall out of step developmentally, with Gerald moving ahead and me stumbling behind?

Our dance would require some new, intricate steps. We chose to bring a new life into the world, hoping that grace and flexibility would accompany our movement into the unknowns of parenthood.

5

And Then There Were Three

Our Son Is Born

> My mother groan'd! my father wept.
> Into the dangerous world I leapt:
> Helpless, naked, piping loud:
> Like a fiend hid in a cloud.
>
> —*W. Blake*[1]

A crisp, urgent voice called me out of my unconscious stupor.

"Madame! Madame! Wake up. You have a boy."

I fought for focus. Where was I? The grip of darkness pulled me back into oblivion.

"Madame!" the nurse insisted again. "Wake up. You have a baby boy."

So that was it. They'd taken my baby out of me. I was empty. A boy? I wondered why she bothered with irrelevant information.

"Is the baby all right?" I mumbled.

"Oh yes. You have a beautiful baby boy."

"But is he all right?" I demanded.

"Yes, yes. Everything is all right."

Reassured, I drifted off again. They soon roused me to deliver a note from Gerald. He had been at home, imagining that things were going slowly; not until he phoned the hospital at the appointed hour did he learn of the cesarean. He rushed over immediately only to find me in the "shockroom" (intensive care) and officially inaccessible. Neither he nor his flowers could reach me. Hurriedly he scrawled a note.

> Sara my lover! Bravo! The baby's doing well, they tell me. And you're a real hero! All my thanks and love! Now I hear you've got an incision, too. Oh well, we know they heal. Be strong and of good courage. Our Lord is watching over us. The son you brought into this world is more precious than any passing pain could earn. I can hardly contain myself for the tumult of love, wonder, and praise. All my love, Gerald.

Still groggy and in increasing pain, I felt far less than euphoric. The nurse's reassurances about our baby no longer convinced me. Her manner was too sweet, too patronizing. Surely she wasn't telling me everything.

And then suddenly, marvelously, Gerald was in the room. In his resourceful way, he had managed to sneak in unobserved. I poured out my anxiety about the panic and flurry before the operation, the erratic heartbeat, the agitated doctors and their hasty decision for surgical intervention.

"Please call our doctor," I begged him. "Find out for sure that all is well with our son."

Gerald, rather faint from the shock of it all, was then brusquely ushered from the room.

I soon discovered that mothers who have undergone

cesarean sections in that hospital are routinely required to recuperate for 48 hours before seeing their babies. The next two days were filled with pain, confusion, and anxiety. My doctor gave me perfunctory, crisp reassurances, implying that everything was in fine shape. I didn't believe him. I thought him too abrupt and not forthcoming with details. I felt that I had a right to know the reasons strong enough for this drastic intervention.

During the first night I rang for the nurse, hoping she would assist in turning me over since pain strapped me down in one position. I lay in a pool of blood. Nobody came. "I'm going to bleed to death!" I thought, coolly calculating my helplessness. "This is intensive care and I'm bleeding to death." After about 15 minutes, a nurse appeared. She took one look and ran for the doctor. He gave me a shot without explanation, presumably to stop the bleeding.

For two days I lay attached to tubes and unable to get out of bed. I don't recall ever feeling so utterly dependent on others for my basic needs. I heard babies crying in the nursery and knew one was mine, but I was powerless to do anything about it.

I was dependent on the nurses' ministrations and small kindnesses. I was also victim to an intolerably insensitive medical system that enacts outrageous restrictions simply for its own convenience.

In saying this, I lay no particular blame on the Yugoslavs themselves. They have come a long way in their medical care with limited resources since World War II left their land a shambles. My quarrel is rather with a particular mind-set found in many hospitals in many countries. Such thinking maximizes concern for efficient functioning and minimizes care for the mother's and baby's emotional well-being in the process. I had chosen to stay for the birth in Yugoslavia, knowing that there were some restrictions I did not appreciate. I hadn't anticipated the extent to which I would feel unable to control my birthing and childcare.

One considerate doctor dressed Gerald in a doctor's white uniform on the second day so that he could visit me at my bedside. The disguise was to help evade a rule forbidding husbands in the maternity ward. The same doctor also allowed Gerald to view our son in the nursery, a "privilege" not otherwise granted until baby and mother are released from the hospital.

Finally I too was favored with the opportunity to meet this stranger who had been so intimate with me these many months. On the second day following delivery the doctor ordered nurses to bring me my baby. He warned me that the baby might not care to nurse: his lip was still scabbed and sore from the forceps.

Forceps? Oh.

Then they brought my little bundle—wrapped tight in swaddling white, looking for all the world like a red-faced mummy. He cried in my arms.

"May I nurse him?"

"Oh no! Nursing time is at 3:00."

They couldn't be serious. But they were! In a moment my son was gone again, whisked back to the nursery. The hour hand crawled sluggishly toward the appointed hour. I readied myself, my heart pounding with eagerness.

In walked the pediatrician.

"Madame, I'm afraid you're too weak to nurse your baby," he chided.

"Indeed I am not," I objected. "I am very able to nurse my baby."

"Oh, but you don't have any milk yet," he continued.

"I have colostrum, and that is filled with good things for my baby." He promptly squeezed my breast, and several drops of clear liquid oozed out.

"But nursing will make your uterus hurt." He was stubborn.

"Those pains are a positive sign that my uterus is contracting and shrinking back to normal size." I was stubborn.

"You know everything!" he sighed, throwing up his arms. Abruptly he turned and walked out of the room.

In two minutes I had my tiny son. With tears of relief I nestled him against my breast. Little Joseph Alexander latched on like a pro and drank with great gusto, in spite of his bloody lip. While touching him, unwrapping him (much to the dismay of the nurse), looking into his dark eyes, and watching the muscles of his face tell stories, I slowly accustomed myself to the truth: he was indeed a healthy, whole baby. Thank you, Good Shepherd!

More of my fears were laid to rest several days later when another doctor, who had assisted in the delivery, gave me (at my request) a fuller medical explanation of the event. In detail he explained that the C-section had been necessary, and that it had been in time. (I was so relieved that our fundamental medical needs had been adequately provided for that it wasn't until much later that I became enraged at the events prior to the surgery and at their use of forceps. I will never know because of the confusion surrounding the incident whether the surgery could have been avoided.)

And then there were eleven days of required recuperation in hospital, eleven days of separation from my baby for long periods of time. What a way for a newborn to start life! And what a way to begin parenthood!

I had definitely been naively overconfident about bringing off a natural, normal delivery. I have learned the hard way that there is so much that can go wrong and so much joy when everything *does* go right. Giving birth (albeit not "naturally") was the most encompassing emotional and physical experience of my life. Less naive than before, I was to view my second pregnancy both more confidently and more cautiously.

Joseph was alive and well, and we were overjoyed. The fetal heart monitor made it possible to pick up signs of distress and the doctors took measures they deemed necessary in time to save our baby. Had Joseph been born in an earlier century, he may not have survived.

Throughout most of Europe 200 years ago, an infant had only one chance in four of surviving birth and childhood.[2] And 400 years ago the chances were still slimmer, with recurring waves of famine and plague. Isolated inventions and discoveries (pasteurization of milk, knowledge of what causes malnutrition, fetal heart monitors, and much more) blend together in a stream of improvements that increase an infant's chances of survival.

Birth is an enormously meaningful and emotionally charged ordeal. Women are increasingly resisting the dehumanizing effects that machines and restrictive hospital environments have on the birthing experience. "Natural" delivery, on the other hand, has sometimes been romanticized as though everything that happens without human interference is benign. Tornadoes and cancers and birth anomalies, however, show another face of nature. One errs by going to either extreme. All mechanical and efficient is hardly humane. All natural and homey is hardly smart. To most men and women the important thing is to have a healthy baby, hopefully in a pleasant and supportive environment. Whatever contributes to this is most truly human.

After eleven long, long days, Gerald and I elatedly walked out of the hospital with baby Joseph finally in our charge. It was a bitterly cold, white day in January. Gingerly we carried our treasure over icy sidewalks and steps to his first real home. At long last we could touch, caress, ogle, and gloat to our hearts' content. With our babe in arms we exulted in the miracle of newborn life that has awed humankind for millennia. Long-forgotten lullabies welled up within us. Memories of the deepest attachments we felt in childhood flooded over us. We both felt an intense desire to nurture this little being, to do all in our power to surround him with love. Birthing our child abruptly initiated us into a new world of awareness.

Unfortunately, despite all that is said and written about parenthood, every new parent starts from scratch. We all have to learn on the job. It takes weeks, months, even years to become parents in our thoughts, feelings, and abilities. The rhythms and priorities of our lives change in the most profound and the most trivial of ways.

My life was thrown off balance by this new dependent being, and I wondered if we would *ever* establish a new equilibrium. The most simple daily routines became elaborate productions. Any patterns that I had enjoyed before were shattered. I now lived in the rhythms of another's life. My entire schedule needed continually to be adjusted according to the baby's unpredictable wakings and feedings. If dinner was only half-prepared when he awoke, dinner waited. If I'd just jumped into the tub when he began to yell, the bath waited. I began to throw a flurry of activity into the few moments just after he'd gone to sleep, knowing that most things would remain undone if I delayed or dallied in "frivolous" nonessentials.

It wasn't long before I felt physically and emotionally spent and wanted to be taken care of myself. I wanted to be held, rocked, and "babied" too. Like many new parents in today's transient society, we lived far away from our extended family network. We had few loving adult relationships where there was a no-strings-attached give and take. I missed my mother more than at any other time in my life. It made me distinctly uncomfortable to suddenly be so dependent on my husband. I needed to turn increasingly to him when fatigue and uncertainty engulfed me.

Tension between my self-preservation and maternal feelings increased with each day. No human being with an ounce of self-awareness can unceasingly answer another being's demands without flashes of rebellion. There were times when I was overwhelmed by the miracle of minute fingers and the softness of a brand-new cheek against mine. In those euphoric moments the weight of love for my baby was almost too great to bear. Yet, at other times I felt undone by the baby's demands, out of control of my life, and immobilized by fatigue.

I began to sense that my whole day was spent perpetuating progeny. Had I become a mere link in a chain of survival with no life to live myself? Our baby's tight handclasp and satisfied chortling during nursing tugged at my heart. Yet many of those nursings broke into my sleep, robbing me of essential relief and guaranteeing that I would be fatigued for one more day of endless days. I found his messy diaper offensive and an outright affront to basic human decency. I teetered on an edge of ambivalence between raw-nerved resentment and tender love.

We had chosen to begin our family at this time in our lives, in lieu of professional involvement for me. Very few attractive work opportunities were available to me in our Yugoslav setting. I had thought it a good time to devote energies to the demands of small children, in the hope that when we returned to the United States I could again be free to pursue further studies.

Even so, I was reluctant to be defined by this new "mother-housewife" identity. Had I compromised my dreams, my sense of self as gifted by God for ministry? Was I forced to choose between motherhood and freedom, motherhood and creativity, motherhood and self-fullfillment?

Child care responsibilities abruptly expelled me from the world of adult interchanges, of relative independence, to a life bogged down with near total concentration on the needs of an infant. I continually subordinated my needs to those of my child. I feared that this little being was literally sucking the life out of me, draining me of vitality and motivation.

Morbid visions filled my mind—a green leaf slowly turning brown and blowing away; a boat helplessly caught in the current, rushing toward a waterfall. One "comforter" wrote that he perceived me now as a trapped butterfly with clipped wings. Some cheerful commiseration!

A lot of housework is repetitive, boring, and never-ending, no matter how valiantly the commercials for floor wax try to glorify it. Scant recognition and rare appreciation make it even less palatable. There are those who rhapsodize about fragrant laundry and fresh apple pie. They go on to claim that they enjoy the "pure joys" of homemaking. Show me a purely joyful housewife and I'll bet she either has hired help or is well beyond the spilled cereal, runny-nosed, interrupted night phase of child care.

I frankly do not find myself breaking forth into song while dumping mounds of reeking diapers into the washer and scrubbing dried food from the high chair. More objectively, it appears that women who are relatively contented with housework usually have taken some domestic task and raised it to a creative art, or they have plenty of leisure time, or they are able to share extensively in their husband's work.[3] Above all, women who are happiest at home clearly know that it is *the children*, not the housework, that deserve their best energies.

Being a full-time homemaker has many satisfactions, but scrubbing dirty floors is not an outstanding one. The major rewards come from relationships: mothering, partnering in marriage, creatively making a home a haven for loved ones. Other aspects of homemaking are necessary, but admittedly not satisfying. Nonetheless, many women feel "one down" when they've decided to stay home full time.

There are those who think an idiot could make a good housewife and mother. After all, it doesn't take any intelligence to scrub toilets and wipe food smears from a baby's face. Others consider housework and mothering to be so worthwhile that they encourage women to devote their entire lives to these activities. Being a housewife is sometimes heralded as the Christian woman's highest calling. What's going on here? Is scrubbing basement steps more noble than chairing a board meeting? Perhaps paying someone else to shine your windows in order to spend more time with your family is more worthy of adulation.

Surely a balanced, sane perspective exists somewhere, perhaps in the lofty philosophical minds of the coolly sophisticated. But a young mother, unraveling under the stress, is hardly capable of sorting through all the "shoulds."

She "should" be an ever present parent, an eternally patient mother, a superb entertainer, a comforting supportive wife, an excellent housekeeper. All of this is unbearably heavy for a young woman badly in need of a healthy dose of mothering herself.

And then our young mother scrambles to restore some order to her upset cart, only to be told that she "should" really pursue her career again. She is encouraged to get out of the house and to fulfill herself as a "working woman." For the woman undone by her new mothering responsibilities, it sometimes appears that the only solution is to run back to the job market, since the feeding of children and the nourishing of families receives scant public praise.

I've felt embarrassed, guilty, even apologetic when confronted with, "Is that all you do?" (You are on duty 24 hours each day, continually in a whirlwind of activity, and they ask, "Is that all?" The audacity!) They imply, "What a waste of your wonderful education." But on what grounds?

Homemaking and marriage *are not* enough! I fully agree. I am a fool if I think I can derive all my self-respect and satisfaction from these roles. But that's not the point. No one can derive total fulfillment in any particular role. Anyone who argues that fulfillment cannot be found at home, and then rhapsodizes about finding guaranteed fulfillment on the job is equally foolhardy.

Militant feminists have assumed that any woman who has the opportunity would choose to be employed. The picture of the average American housewife's life painted by these feminists is as distorted as their view of the average employed woman's world is romanticized. Many women who combine families and careers report that instead of the hoped-for feelings of challenge and excitement, their dual roles bring frustration and tension. Some eventually come to the conclusion that their job equals money, nothing more. Fulfillment still eludes them.[4] In the same vein, traditionalists who argue that housekeeping should be supremely fulfilling are wearing blinders. Housekeeping and childcare when seen as an end in themselves are not the key to fulfillment.

No woman is really free unless she can have options. She needs to find her way through all the "shoulds" to a place where she feels able freely to choose to care for her baby and to make space for herself as well. Extreme feminism seems to substitute one form of tyranny for another, insisting that fulfillment is to be found only outside the home. Separating mothers from the daily life of their infants does a disservice to both of them. But isolating frustrated mothers at home with their infants, as traditionalists advocate, without providing adequate support structures or changing structures to better suit their needs, is also a disservice.

I have often been a restless, impatient, and tired mother. The shock of motherhood left me reeling. But all the while I knew I passionately loved my little son and wanted to do all in my power to nourish him into healthy wholesome childhood. Sometimes our baby seemed like an interruption to my growth. Other times his birth and babyhood felt, in a mysterious way, like an essential part of a process that would clarify who I am. At times my child seemed to prevent me from following Christ. On other occasions I felt that I was approaching a fuller understanding of God's incomprehensible work in my life. In the ambivalence of my conflicting feelings I searched for a way in which both my baby's needs for nurture and my need for creative fulfillment could be met.

6

Freedom in a Flash

Insight into True Liberation

I'm Nobody! Who are you?
Are you—Nobody—Too?
Then there's a pair of us?
Don't tell! they'd advertise—you know!

How dreary—to be—Somebody!
How public—like a Frog—
To tell one's name—the livelong June—
To an admiring Bog!

—*Emily Dickinson*[1]

What do you do?" my Dutch guest queried. His question disturbed me. While serving tea and coffee cake, soothing baby Timothy, carrying on a sideways dialogue with two-year-old Joseph's finger puppets, and maintaining a lively conversation with my guests, I grasped frantically for an answer.

Among the three or four things I usually do at once, what

do I *do?* Oh, for a tidy label to neatly define me! I'd like to sum up all my varied interests and activities in one eminent title, so that I could satisfy any inquirer.

I scrambled to find an answer for my guest that might rate, knowing that neither *mother* nor *homemaker* was up to snuff. "I'm trained as a high school teacher . . ." "I've studied theology . . ." "I sell an occasional short story. . . ." And then I balked. Thoroughly incensed at my repeated sellout to the status quo, I simply said, "I enjoy my family."

He looked at me blankly.

"I *do*. I really enjoy my family!"

The conversation flitted to other more "significant" topics. Parental jobs are low on conversational appeal.

I'm often asked, "Do you work?" I know full well the presupposition and good intentioned interest that spurs such a question, but every time I hear it I feel like *growling*. The term "working mother" is absolutely bankrupt, in denoting only those simultaneously employed outside the home. What mother isn't working, day in and day out?

Timothy Ivan, our second son, was born during a four-month leave to the United States. Joseph eagerly welcomed his new playmate home, but on discovering that Timothy could not walk, talk, or play, he asked in exasperation, "Well, what *can* he do?"

We advised patience, to which Joseph sternly replied, "I'll teach him to grow up!" (It was a relief to know we would have help this time around!)

Three weeks after Timothy's birth, we returned to our work and study in Yugoslavia. Days and nights agonizingly twisted into each other with Timothy showing a penchant for late night colic. For a long three months we lived in a wee one-room apartment, waiting until a larger place became available. Joseph slept just a yard away from Timothy, who slept a yard away from us. Fortunately, Joseph's deep repose remained intact through Timothy's nightly serenades.

Fatigue hounded me continually. Many a night as I nursed Timothy I felt quite literally like a "living sacrifice." Just getting to the end of the day seemed a formidable impossibility. And then a night of piercing yells for mother's milk stretched ahead, offering little relief. No longer could I nap while Joseph slept in the afternoon because Timothy usually chose that time to squall.

At 10:00 one evening I wrote: "This is the first quiet, solitary, moment I've had all day. Earlier this eve Joseph asked me, 'Wanna 'lax, Mama?' He begged me, 'Mama, come 'lax.' He stretched out on the couch, hoping that would suffice in place of his going to bed." Indeed it would not suffice; I desperately needed some time to " 'lax" all by myself!

So how could I give testimony for our Dutch guest of joy and satisfaction with my family preoccupations? I was trapped in a drab, mildewed basement room with two insatiable little codgers in a foreign country—the height of masochistic martyrdom. Why didn't I put my foot down and declare that I'd had it? Why didn't I complain that I'd much rather be elsewhere, doing something *worthy* of my talents?

"All children have a touch of magic about them," says Fynn in *Mister God, This Is Anna.* "Like some mysterious lens they seem to have the capacity to focus the light in the darkest and gloomiest places. . . . They can and do, if you give them half a chance, make a dent in the toughest armour of life."[2]

The miracle burst on me in a momentary flash of acceptance, the miracle of a relationship with a child that I wouldn't trade for the world. When a little two-year-old throws his arms around my neck and whispers, "Mama, I love you *too* much," my defenses dissolve. In striving for big, important moments, I had overlooked the beauty of the little ones. Little moments crammed with life are all we have, after all.

Life is too short, I decided, to wait for some distant dream while disregarding the potential of the present. I decided to embrace NOW, and savor each moment. Perhaps with a prominent professional position I would no longer need to scramble to define myself and my work, but henceforth I would not ignore the beauty and love that surround me.

I could no longer be captive to a concept of liberation that focused on activities outside the home alone. Paycheck equality and professional opportunity for women are a noble cause, but my liberation would have to be different.

I regret that the term "liberation" is loosely used as if it were synonymous with being employed. Most people are not liberated by virtue of what they have to do for a living. Career development simply does not equal or produce liberation. It is absolutely phony to esteem a person's worth in accord with professional and career achievements.

Some of my peers, however, were becoming teachers, counselors, psychologists, and communicators. I could not always draw the comparisons in ways that made my choices seem more glamorous or immediately rewarding. Tensions would build up, especially in conversations with friends or family members who might ask how it feels when one of my closest friends is nearing completion of her Ph.D.

Shortly after one of our visits to the United States, I wrote my friend:

I'm angry with the assumption that yours is *a priori* the better, more liberated choice. I'm sure you share my anger at
that mind-set. So my argument isn't with you or your calling, but with the false stereotypes fueled by concepts of
"liberation" and "success" that are very un-Christlike. I
have been defensive at times, and still am when people
refuse to redefine their categories. I don't see living in and
for the kingdom as necessarily separate from developing
professional skills. Far from it. *Rather, those skilled to serve
with an unpretentious humility are so very needed here and
everywhere.*

Rather than measuring our self-worth in relation to the
economic system or to professional status, we can take an inner measure. Whether we are free-lance artists, pastors, cor-
poration presidents, parents, or farmers, the soul-searching is
the same. Where do we stand in relationship to God? How
does our chosen vocation mesh with the eternal verities of
almighty God? Knowing *whose* we are brings *who* we are
into clearer focus. Authentic liberation does not come from
an organization or a movement. Liberation is a *state of the
mind* in which a woman comes to view herself as Jesus
Christ sees her: a person made in God's image.[3] God wants
to make us free! When in step with the Liberator's dance of
release, we can freely offer all of our talents and gifts back to
their Creator, in whose keeping they will flourish.

The good news is that a woman finds her identity in her
love relationship with Jesus Christ. The answers given by
traditionalists and secular feminists to the problem of a
woman's identity have not meshed with Jesus' message of
release and liberation. We cannot find our true identities in
roles, in careers, through our children, or through our husbands. Only in an unparalleled relationship with a God
whose name is Love can we find the liberation we seek.

One day as I struggled to understand God's work of liberation in my life, I found this psalm and claimed it as a gift from God to me:

> My heart is not proud, O Lord,
>   My eyes are not haughty;
> I do not concern myself with great matters
>   or things too wonderful for me.
> But I have stilled and quieted my soul;
>   like a weaned child with its mother,
>   like a weaned child is my soul within me.
>
> —Psalm 131:1, 2

We are God's children above all, and God has set us free. Within that liberty there is no single way for each of us to serve our God. There is no neatly defined woman's role to encapsulate all of our different needs, gifts, and interests. The diversity gives me liberty to continue as both a committed Christian and a feminist.

As my child led me, I began to sense that motherhood is an adventure. Yes, child care is enormously time-consuming and frequently isolating. But to my growing amazement, being with children and learning to live within their rhythms brought exquisite joy also. The instigators of so much chaos around my feet were also providing some of the shining highlights of my life.

I haven't yet met the mother who looks back on the early days of motherhood and smugly declares, "It was a lark! I loved every minute." But I did write in my journal after the conversation with my Dutch friend, "I'm beyond the stage of apologizing for having children. I wouldn't trade them for anything."

Perhaps I had weathered most of those ominous warnings

that cloud the horizon for a potential mother: "It's going to change your life; you'll never really recover the same intimacy with your husband; you'll never be able to go out to eat or see a movie on a moment's notice again; your career will suffer; you'll ruin your figure; you'll need to lower your living standards; your egalitarian marriage will fall into the patriarchal pits."

To make the case for children in spite of such pessimistic rumblings is almost impossible without sounding sentimental or tradition-bound. Most of the joys of parenting are indescribable and unanticipated. The rewards involve a new quality of love, so powerful that it almost certainly has a biological basis. Nobody can quite prepare us for the impact of a baby's fresh promise of life. Nobody can tell us how happy our child will make us. Nobody can predict the joy that bursts on us as we watch a new being awaken to the world. Nobody can foretell how much our children will love us, forgive us, and push us to grow up with them. It frightens me now to think that in my glorification of careers and my ignorance of children, I might so easily have missed a central and lasting satisfaction of my life.

I still have days when everything my childless friends do makes my own work seem pale and insignificant by comparison. On such days I wonder, did I make the right choice? Why do I feel so inconsequential and small? A professor acquaintance of ours ran into some professional snags and jested, "It's enough to make you want to go home and have a baby!"

I wanted to retort, "Sure! You think having babies is a cinch and a grand cop-out for the weak who can't cut it in the real world. Try it, friend! Then see if you can pooh-pooh it."

I do want to affirm that a woman's decision not to have children may be rooted in other, more worthy considerations. There are many options in our day for those who do not feel called to parenting. Just as Christians may choose celibacy, so potential parents may choose to remain childless to better serve their Christ and fulfill their vocations. Persons who take this path are not necessarily rejecting children nor trading them for selfish fulfillment. Some, at least, in choosing to remain childless are enabled to work single-mindedly in a way that those who have familial responsibilities cannot. Child-free persons are an invaluable asset to the body of believers. They are uniquely gifted with reservoirs of energy and vision on which we all depend.

Whether we choose to raise children or not, each of us is bound to experience some moments of regret, along with the corresponding joys. Once that decision is made, however, we do well not to look back. A child does not deserve to be viewed as an impediment or a roadblock. She or he is indeed a gift, and has a strong claim on the best marriage arrangement and supportive environment we can facilitate for a child's care.

When I became a mother, I most wanted to establish a high quality of family life. This prime function of life is to be *enjoyed*. I didn't intend merely to survive or endure until I could move on to other more "noteworthy" pursuits. No! *Now,* I decided, is the time to cherish the adventure of being a mother to my children. *Now* is the time to selfishly claim one unique aspect of being woman and, by choice, primary nurturer. *Now* is the moment of happiness shared with two bright-eyed boys, whose contagious glee buoys up my spirits even as their wails drag me down.

"Mama, are you glad that you are a mother?" Joseph

abruptly asked me one day. I mustered all the faith I could manage (Lord, help my unbelief) and answered, "Yes, Joseph. There's nothing else I'd rather be doing than being mother to two fine little boys." He snuggled contentedly against me.

Women throughout history have been praised and feared for their reproductive capabilities. The body is only one part of the female reality, however. Similarly, motherhood is not the sole definition of what it means to be woman. A woman is a total person, with heart and mind, will and abilities. In addition to the fruit of her womb, she has the fruit of the Spirit and the fruit of her mind to offer the world.[4]

After receiving an inner assurance that domesticity and parenting aren't the totality of who I am, I more gladly and willingly chose to be a homemaker for a season. Life has a special meaning at each stage. Why should I resist this phase simply because it doesn't include the benefits of the next phase? I am thankful for the privilege of these few years at home with our children. Knowing their total dependency is temporary, I can embrace parenting with renewed vigor.

Some mothers and other women are finding their way into the job market after a domestic time out. The schools are welcoming many of us into preparation for second careers. Professors have noted that such students are often more informed, experienced, and committed than young people fresh from previous schooling.

Parenthood is a practicum with valuable lessons that eluded me while I walked the halls of academia. The tangible and creative work of child care offers a healthy antidote to intangible academics. By balancing hand work with mind work, I can maintain an equilibrium.

Even some feminists have at times linked personal

development exclusively to public roles, implying that husbands have the real opportunities to grow while wives are stuck with the care of little ones. This is mistaken on two counts at least: first, in wrongly presuming that the nurturer is not growing, and second, in endorsing a social order that values "masculine" public priorities more than relationships.

Shared parenting can provide new growth in the nurturing father and the nurturing mother alike. Fathers grow immeasurably from living intimately with children and being responsible for their daily care. In nurturing a small child, adults stand to learn as much about themselves as they do about the infant.[5] We might even say that as we nurture children, we are in turn nurtured by them.

Sometimes we think we will never live through this child-centered phase. They drive us crazy and we think we're cracking up. But then something happens to let us know that we're changed persons for having survived them; perhaps even better persons!

Caring for children brings us face to face with ourselves in revealing ways. There is an ancient notion that you find yourself through another self, especially when helping to create another. We each spend a lifetime in birthing ourselves, one way or another. I resolved to use even pregnancy, birth, and child care in giving birth to myself. We aren't squandering ourselves by sharing life with eternally spirited little people. Abundant maturity and wisdom become ours in return, "a good measure, pressed down, shaken together and running over."

"Many parents stress what *they* do for their children," noted Chicago TV anchorwoman Susan Anderson, "but children really do so much more for you. [My daughter has] made me more responsible, more mature. She's given a real ballast to my life. Children are a great leveler. They show you what's important." Anderson commented that her work is stimulating, immediate, and glamorous. Her baby daughter, she said, is the opposite of that. "She is permanent and she responds to love and warmth, not power and status. She provides a balance in my life."[6]

My father often recited the words from Emily Dickinson's poem, "I'm nobody! Who are you?" When someone in the family felt let down by failure or missed an honorable mention we gave solace to each other in Dickinson's comforting lines, quoted at the outset of this chapter. Somehow we knew that in being "nobody" we could find peace, and ultimately, freedom. What matters is not credential or fame, or even success as a parent, but a calm acceptance of our limitations.

Thomas Merton has said:

> Our Christian destiny is, in fact, a great one: but we cannot achieve greatness unless we lose all interest in being great. For our idea of greatness is illusory, and if we pay too much attention to it we will be lured out of the peace and stability of the being God gave us, and seek to live in a myth we have created for ourselves. It is, therefore, *a very great thing to be little, which is to say: to be ourselves.*[7]

After recognizing my limitations I felt free to take what I *did* have and make it a treasure to be prized! As a mother, I felt compelled to accept the inevitable constraints of parenting and to use them as an invaluable experience of growth. I lay claim to motherhood as an integrating and rewarding experience, rich with lessons to be learned.

Part II
Pedagogy of Parenthood

7

Responsibility

A Gentle Yoke, A Light Burden

> One who is content with what he has,
> and who accepts the fact that
> he inevitably misses very much in life,
> is far better off than one who has much more
> but who worries about all he may be missing.
> For we cannot make the best of what we are
> if our hearts are always divided
> between what we are and what we are not.
>
> —*Thomas Merton*[1]

A recurring dream haunted my sleep in the first months after Joseph's birth. It had me blissfully going downtown to a movie or a concert. Hours later as I sat absorbed in the show, panic suddenly paralyzed me: I had forgotten my baby! My heart crumbled. In great fear I rushed home, hoping that nothing dreadful had happened to our helpless infant. Oh, how could I be so heartless? How could I have forgotten him? Surely he was shrieking in an agony of abandonment.

I awoke from this dream relieved to find my baby sleeping peacefully beside me. But the residue of fear remained. Would a momentary lapse into my carefree pre-parental state of consciousness actually be possible? How could a person who had only been accountable for her own comings and goings suddenly become responsible for a round-the-clock vigil over a helpless baby? It involved nothing less than an altered state of consciousness, an upheaval in my psychological makeup.

No advance warnings about a baby's impact could have prepared me for the tricks my psyche would play. The burden of care for this little being overloaded my circuits. No! I cried. I can't bear the weight of this child's clutches on my constancy. What if I'm not constant? What if my so-called instincts don't serve me well, and he slips out of my arms, drowns in his bath, or smothers in his blankets? Worse yet, what if my mind does a fluke and I forget that he is waiting for me, Me, and only ME?

In Isaiah 49:15, God is compared to a lactating woman who could *perhaps* forget her offspring. "Can a mother forget the baby at her breast and have no compassion on the child she has borne? Though she may forget, I will not forget you!"

It is reassuring to know that God is completely trustworthy, and it is only human to admit that we are not! As parents we are entrusted with a sacred and immensely heavy responsibility to care adequately for our helpless offspring. We are expected to be and want to be *completely* trustworthy. But we know in our hearts that we are fallible. We are human.

During those first months I was reluctant for Gerald to leave for any length of time. I hadn't minded being by myself before. Now, when Gerald's work took him away I urgently wanted someone else in the house with me. I didn't want to bear the responsibility of infant care alone.

Babies are totally demanding beings. And there is nothing casual about a first child. You can't take anything about his or her care for granted. You question everything. Is she too hot or too cold? Is his belly too distended or too flat? Are her stools too yellow or too green? Do I hold him too often? Is she crying too frequently or should I allow her to cry more often?

There is no end to the new specialties in which you are expected to be an instant and confident expert. You give, give, and give—anything to keep ahead of the towering wave of guilt that will come crashing down as soon as someone insinuates that you've been negligent.

I remember well the recriminations that showered on me when I allowed my baby to suck his fingers with contentment (he preferred them to his thumb). Many a person felt compelled to pull Joseph's fingers forcefully from his mouth, with sharp reprimands, suggesting that his fingers would either become flabby and misshapen or that he would die of some dire infection from germ-ridden hands. One woman declared that unless a baby cried thirty minutes per day his chest and shoulders would never develop properly. Another suggested that I nurse him as soon as he merely whimpered. One person announced that the way I let my baby's head flop against my shoulder endangered his neck and back; another remarked on how flexible and durable babies' bodies are.

Sometimes when my best efforts to comfort did nothing

to soothe my distraught baby, I'd abruptly put him down
and leave the room in a huff. Let him scream if he must. I'd
had it! Then I'd return, subdued, to rock him with renewed
fervor, afraid that my anger had wounded his spirit.

Many a morning when the baby's yells broke out in the
wee hours, I clung to my pillow, pulling the covers closer
around me. "Oh please, please Joseph, go back to sleep."
Once in a blissful blue moon he did drop off again, and I felt
heaven smiling on my sleep. Far more often, though, he
insisted that I drag my body out of bed and stagger bleary-
eyed into another morning. And what awaited me? Another
day of sacrificing myself to care for his needs.

As I reflected on the way my baby was sapping my
energies, fundamental questions about life stared into my
drooping eyes. For whom am I living this life? Was all my
training and experience mere preparation for confinement to
baby care? Are freedom and responsible commitment to my
child in conflict?

For most of us, whether we admit it or not, the central
theme of our life seems unambiguous: self-fulfillment.
There is nothing unusual about self-centered feelings. Who
doesn't want a great deal of self-gratification in marriage
(and in all relationships, for that matter)? That is why Angela Barron McBride sees having a baby as such a *turning
point*.

It takes plenty of reorientation, notes McBride, to get
used to being selfless toward our children. Living with
children in a loving give-and-take fashion requires major ad-
justment in our self-understanding because it is the first time
most of us have been called upon to be truly unselfish.[2]

One new father writes that his dominant emotion at this
turning point was fear. After seeing his firstborn, he re-

marked: "I am of a generation that has made self-indulgence a kind of secular religion. I looked down at that baby, and suddenly I felt that a whole part of my life had just ended, been cut off, and I was beginning something for which I had no preparation."[3]

Social critic Michael Novak observed in 1976 that children are not a welcome responsibility now, for to have children is, clearly, to cease being a child oneself. The courage to marry and raise a family, he claimed, presupposes a (presently unfashionable) willingness to grow up.[4] Metamorphosis into selflessness, however, is a change that can have high costs, and is never complete.

Most of us parents, holding our newborn, feel unspeakable conviction that our baby *matters*. Mobility, career, and other personal adventures lose in significance. We begin painstakingly to change our priorities, to take this new dependent relationship into account. We realign our lives, summoning every ounce of selflessness that we can muster.

Some simple answers are urged upon us today. Why change our style of life? Parents are for giving birth, and the rest is the responsibility of experts and institutions. Some predict that utopia will have arrived when every mother and father has a job in an office and every child has a place in a day-care center.[5]

This brings us to the fundamental question underlying our discussion of responsibility and freedom. Can parents give their babies something that no one else can provide?

One mother observes, "I have come to realize that there is nothing I am doing in the world of work—or that I ever will do no matter how high I go—that can't be done by somebody else. But nobody else can do for my children what I can do."[6]

Especially in the first years of a child's life, few substitutes can match a good mothering relationship in providing for a child's emotional and cognitive development.[7] In later stages of development, the child's environment and group experiences outside the home take on greater significance. However, language skills and personality formation belong to those first years. If a child has a cheerful mother with her during her first five years at home, she has an advantage. However, the trusted, responsive adult who is always around the child does not have to be the child's mother.[8]

In *Every Child's Birthright: In Defense of Mothering*, Selma Fraiberg defines "mothering" as the nurturing of the human potential of babies to love, to trust, and to bind themselves to human partnerships. Fraiberg decries the devaluation of parental nurturing and commitment to babies in our society. She notes that children's capacity to commit themselves in love and in human community is diminished or depleted when extraordinary circumstances like disaster, hardship, or indifference deprive them of a mother or a mother substitute. The number of such children, unfortunately, is growing in our society.[9]

A baby can suffer "maternal deprivation" even when physical care is quite adequate, if at the same time that child does not develop a *focused personal bond* with a particular person. By providing repeated experiences of contact and comfort, pleasure and attention, the mothering person aids the baby's grasp of the world and sense of self. The baby whose needs are met by a constantly shifting set of people and places may well develop a shaky self-identity. At least one person must be predictably familiar to the infant, or the little one will lack emotional discrimination, with ominous results. Babies who are well-loved, cared for, and remembered will in turn develop their own capacities for memory and attention.[10]

A child's love is not instinctive, not even a heritable trait; it is largely a love that is born of love. A child loves because he or she is loved.[11] The exuberance, the smiles, the excited kicking of a baby are not mere abilities in its innate repertoire, but evidence that the baby's human partners have given him or her a sense of trust and pleasure.

I used to wonder when our babies would manage to return those magic words, "I love you." This expression cannot be forced. Will it ever spring forth unsolicited? Every parent awaits the day when the child discovers his capacity to return love. One morning I awoke to the padding of little feet. Barely two years old, Timothy called out on his way to our room: "I'm waking up, Mama. I'm waking up."

He climbed quietly into bed and snuggled under the covers as his parents obstinately clung to their slumbers. Reveling in the reassuring closeness of Mom and Dad, he said gently, almost to himself, "I love you."

"What?" I asked groggily.

"I love you," he repeated. I drowsily basked in his first spontaneous verbalization of that emotion. Would that we could always be worthy of his fond regard.

The more I understood that the course of a lifetime is set by that day-to-day, moment-by-moment nurture of our child in his first years, the more I embraced my mothering as a serious vocation. I wanted to stay home with my sons because their nurture is too great a task to pass off to someone who wouldn't care as much as I do. I wanted to be the one who would hear their first words, and see them proudly take their first steps. No other care givers could feel the fantastic joy Gerald and I knew when our son began to draw crazy scrawls and label them with whatever struck his fancy. Who else would treasure each new development from day to day with the same glee we expressed? Who else would interpret our child's distress signals with the same sensitivity and concern that we expect of ourselves? The idea that today's job market and institutional arrangements are peopled with ranks of staffers who will be just as affectionate, responsive, and concerned for a baby as its own parents—this is a barren, political notion.[12]

Is three or four years really too high a price to pay for ensuring that a new little person will have a secure, confident sense of self, and thus be free later to forge out on his or her own? The universal fears in childhood include the fear of being abandoned, or being unloved, or getting hurt. It seems well worth a parent's while to be there at the beginning, having as much influence as possible on all that potential and vulnerability! Women and men *who have a choice,* who are economically and emotionally able to do this, are laying an invaluable foundation for their child's future by caring for that child themselves in the most formative stages. Few jobs or professions can offer the parents anything more important to them in the years to come than what can be accomplished in a close relationship with their child in the first years of life.

The choice is ours, either to embrace this most creative job and give it our best, or to see ourselves as mere slaves toiling away in household drudgery. In actuality, one of the few remaining free professions is that of a homemaker. There are many advantages in being at home full time. We can go barefoot, listen to music, wear comfortable clothes, take a walk on impulse if the birds and balmy air beckon, relax our minds, and pray as we work. We can thank God for a house to clean and food to prepare. We need not squeeze our children into the fringes of a frenzied day. Although people in the job market are considered to be "in the action," and those at home are "out of it," we can aggressively redefine what the real action is. The whole world is not at the office. The world throbs all around us—at the park, in the museum, on the street corner, in our homes. The *real action* is where close human relationships are given preeminence!

Responsibility as a parent is probably the greatest task a person will ever face. Many would affirm that working to build the best family possible is the greatest contribution one can make to our society, and the greatest fulfillment there can be. I would suggest (with some qualification) that there is little that most men and women do in the work force or even in the arts that is as satisfying or makes as much difference as creating a place of belonging, a place for human companionship.

I have often chafed at home, wondering what I could do in active service to help alleviate the pain and suffering so rampant in our world. This was heightened for me in a recent sermon on Jesus' hard saying in Luke 14:26—"If anyone comes to me and does not hate his father and mother, his wife and children, his brothers and sisters—yes, even his own life, he cannot be my disciple." Prior to becoming a mother of two dependents, I readily accepted this text and recognized that it speaks about ultimate and final loyalties.

This sermon, however, brought me up short. This preacher who prophetically and yet lightly chided us for being so tied to homes and families, was himself single. The call for prophetic sojourners sounded to me for the first time like one more put-down of women or men who stay home in order to create small circles of respite. I wanted to retort, "Where does your admonition leave those of us who are trying to raise secure, peace-loving children? Is all the glorious sacrifice and suffering for Jesus done out there, somewhere far from the home?"

Gerald noted after the sermon that two intertwining themes run throughout the New Testament. One is the tradition of the traveling prophets who cried out for repentance. The other is the commitment to build loving communities. These two traditions complement and correct each other.

I felt somewhat relieved. I see myself as an advocate within the home for social awareness. I view child-rearing as one of the most effective forms of social action. To bring up children who learn compassion for others, who value relationships above the material benefits of a consumptive society, and who can resist the numbing, cheapening influences of the media: this is social action of the first order!

On the other hand, women often hear from male preachers that nurturing children is a woman's highest calling. I object to such a narrow view of calling and such a one-sided view of women. That notion not only implies that all childless women have missed their highest calling; it also insinuates that men have a different highest calling. What might that be? Perhaps preachers would do better to say that nurturing children is a "uniquely sacred task. Period."[13]

One day as our family foursome pursued separate activities, Joseph commented, "Mom, this is a pretty busy and happy house, isn't it?"

I exulted in his sense of well-being. The freedoms I had sacrificed seemed well worth the cost if they enhanced the reality of goodness in my child's self-understanding.

Marriage and parenthood are an assault on the lonely, autonomous ego. Family responsibilities impose humbling, baffling, and frustrating burdens on us. Yet it is precisely such difficulties that are likely to lead us toward true liberation. No longer are we trapped in some lonely private destiny.

The emphasis shifts from our personal freedom to the significance of caring relationships. Maturity and its accompanying liberation are not automatic by-products of turning 21. They gradually accrue, instead, as we deliberately decide for responsible relationships, even when it hurts. We have to choose to grow up. We have to choose what yoke we are willing to bear and be thankful if we find that yoke easy and the burden light.

Once we truly recognize that life is difficult, writes Scott Peck, once we can understand and accept the fact, then life is no longer difficult. Because we have accepted it, the fact that life is difficult no longer matters. Life poses an endless series of problems that call forth our courage and our wisdom, creating more courage and wisdom. Difficulties challenge us to grow both mentally and spiritually.[14]

It is a rare mother who doesn't ever feel like abandoning everything to go off on a Carribean cruise (or some other exotic escape fit to her fancy). Usually Gerald and I fantasize about it together. We possess two powerful and natural desires. We want to love, feed, and care for our family, and we want to escape from its narrow confines. It is hardly ever possible to reconcile both desires completely. One of them must be repressed. To live is to choose, and to choose is always to renounce something.[15]

Right now our main commitment is to our boys. We prize

their well-being more than our own freedom to act out our fantasies. Parenthood is a choice made with the knowledge that we will have to do some hard things, make some sacrifices, even give up some dreams.

Any commitment, whether to career or self-improvement projects of any sort, has its less exciting moments. Where in life can you achieve without some inconvenience? Limitations define the gifts and abilities of every living thing. As parents now we have traded some freedom and mobility for another set of satisfactions which are more private and personal. The mixture of pleasure and pain is part of what it means to be alive.

The focus on freedom in our society often carries an unbiblical connotation. It is used to imply an absence of restraints. For some, to be "liberated" means being free to act on whim, to become infatuated, to be ruled by selfishness.

The biblical concept of freedom is not freedom *from restraints*, but freedom *to serve others*. Galatians 5:1 and 13 make this theme explicit: "It is for freedom that Christ has set us free. Stand firm, then, and do not let yourselves be burdened again by a yoke of slavery ... You ... were called to be free. But do not use your freedom to indulge the sinful nature; rather, serve one another in love."

This question faces every struggling young parent: am I free enough to be responsible? Am I free enough to choose to put another's well-being above my own? Am I free enough to step aside and let another's demands and needs occupy center stage for a time?

To find oneself is not possible without self-denial, contrary to what many so-called liberation advocates would claim. Certain ways of saving one's life are to lose it, while certain ways of losing one's life are to save it. More Christians and feminists must come together in this knowledge.

Biblical feminist Virginia Ramey Mollenkott encourages us to see God in the mundane details of our personal existence. Even the troublesome household chore and the tiring care of children can become an act of worship. She affirms that every person has a ministry. If we have not formally valued our particular form of ministry as an opportunity for constant worship, for constant incarnation of Christ within our sphere of influence, we should begin to look at our life in that light from this moment forward.[16]

Parenting is a sacred ministry worthy of our best gifts. We give without expecting an immediate reward. We love without instantaneous fulfillment. We exist without much special recognition. In so doing we offer our living sacrifice of worship to a God who promises never to forget us or abandon us, but to give us abundant liberty and life. Only in God can we save our life while losing it.

8

Tolerance

Humble and Human After All

My grace is sufficient for you, for my power is made perfect in weakness.
2 Corinthians 12:9.

S tanding in the midst of our living room strewn with blocks, toys, and papers; weaving in and out of a zigzag chat with a friend as my two-year-old loudly insists that he knows best, I am suddenly engulfed in a flash-back. There is prim, punctual, childless me in the midst of another's toy-littered home, wondering why *they* can't keep a tidier house, wondering why *they* permit a child to clamor about monkey-style while we attempt a serious discussion.

As our children grew, my tidy, controlled life frayed badly. Emotions I thought I possessed only in manageable quantities reared their heads with vigor: anger, impatience, exasperation. I who thought I could always cope, simply could not.

Children evoke a range of new emotions in us. They tax

our limits, upset our schedules, demand first priority. They tear apart our homes, throw tantrums in front of our friends, and punch holes in our self-confidence. Those of us who made snide comments about other people's kids and self-righteously quoted from college texts on child development discover this new kid quantity to be much more slippery and unpredictable than we'd expected. We, who had taken potshots at our own parents, now feel uneasy, recognizing our own capacity for mistakes and acknowledging that parents are people, too. We find new appreciation for our peers who are parenting, struggling to lead wholesome lives while coping with interrupted nights and an infinite number of distractions and disruptions.

A baby arrives, clothed in pristine freshness, a bundle of perfection. She should rightfully be placed in the hands of perfect, saintly parents (or so it seemed to me one day as I meditated on my shortcomings). Children deserve the very best! These innocent, trusting, impressionable little cherubs should be given the optimum conditions for flowering into their full potential. Anything less is a travesty of justice. And what kind of caretakers do these brand-new beauties get? They get us! Fallible, fumbling, half-baked adults. We sincerely want to do our best, but being parents somehow shows up the worst in us.

Mothering is the most difficult job I have ever undertaken. The patience, tolerance, wisdom, physical and emotional energy required of a parent in a single day are truly phenomenal! I continually have the sense that I should have more to give, even while showing strengths I didn't know I had.

A mother's hours on duty often add up to 24 per day. The wage is usually atrocious. There are no overtime payments, no weekends or holiday breaks. You get a tea break only if you make the tea yourself.

At present, mothers themselves hardly acknowledge the value or skill of what they do. If they care adequately for their babies, they are only doing what is expected of them. In any other job this same accomplishment would earn significant respect.[1] The psychic burden is almost unbearable for mothers who are repeatedly told what they're doing isn't significant. Their place in national statistics on depression is assured: two or three times as many women as men in the United States are depressed.[2]

The weariest women around are usually mothers of children under four years of age. Most people can't comprehend what a mother's day is like. "All" we do is a few chores around the house and keep the kids. Why do we continually gasp, "I'm so tired!"? We're exhausted at the end of the day and have nothing to show for it. Fatigue dogs us like a low-grade infection. We think we'll never feel rested again.

When I hear non-parents say they are tired I don't believe them, though I usually refrain from an outright snort of disbelief. If you have missed a night to study for exams you can usually look forward to making it up the next night, or at least sleep in on Saturday morning. Parents know that no such makeup night exists for them. No vacation getaway is on the horizon. Nights with two to seven interruptions and broken dreams stretch into the dim distance.

What mother hasn't dreamed at one point of "going over the edge?" At least in relinquishing her sanity she could finally be taken care of herself, after depleting all her resources in caring for someone else.

I know the desperation of having practically no one to

turn to. During our Yugoslav sojourn Gerald's work would sometimes take him away for days at a time. On one such occasion the boys were both sick, and consequently I had little sleep. I was torn between indulging their every demand, and maintaining discipline. When Timothy woke for the seventh time to be nursed, I decided that he had really had enough milk just a short time ago, so I let him cry.

Then, finding his wails intolerable, I finally picked him up after all. Such indecision is guaranteed to create worse problems later on, but in my exhaustion I wasn't blessed with the strength to be consistent. Instead, I felt violent. Had I not been taught self-control, I might have shaken that child and thrown him back into bed. The thought certainly occurred to me.

There is a fine line between self-control and loss of it; parents who truly love their children can nevertheless cross that line sometimes. When I've had more whining than I can stand during the day, my thoughts can turn violent. And if I, with a strong home background and relatively supportive environment, am tempted to such violent outbursts, is it any wonder that so many other parents abuse children? When our children provoke us to extremes so that we want to yell, slap, and kick, it doesn't mean that we are wicked; it does mean that we are *too alone* in child care.

Some of the indignities we face in caring for little children are too much for a gracious response. One Sunday morning, just after I had returned to the United States from Yugoslavia, sudden disaster struck. Gerald was still traveling, and I was in charge of our two boys. I was eager to attend church to meet friends and family whom we hadn't seen for years.

Timothy became ill, throwing up four times all over

himself and his mother. Diarrhea quickly followed. While comforting him in his distress, and trying to determine what beastly germ had attacked my son, I needed to scrap my greatly anticipated morning plans.

Do you collapse in tears under such an onslaught, or blow up in anger? Both! You can also throw propriety and plans to the winds, and slow down to the pace of a child's needs. With the help of Gerald's mother, I survived a five-day vomiting spree on that occasion. Sometimes I cried. Mostly I buttoned my lip and hung on, hoping each day that we had found the cause and could remedy it.

There are days and more days when it is easier to do practically nothing, because the minute I try to do something constructive the baby crawls over and starts begging to be held. And then when he is happily playing he is such a delight to be with that I don't get anything else done either. The most frustrating days are often those in which I have had the greatest expectation of accomplishing many tasks.

Every minute of a day with a toddler is spent trying to control, correct, and corral all that tempestuous energy. Each day throws up new tasks in pleasant persuasion and feeding that precious curiosity. You have to be a human yo-yo to survive. One minute I try to open the door for our two-year-old. He shouts, "No. No! Me do dat!"

Knowing that his tiny hands cannot yet master the knob, I walk away, allowing him to clutch and fumble at it anyway. Soon he is a flailing heap of tears and frustration. So I return and ask if I may help. If I'm lucky I manage a compromise. But the tug-of-war scenario will happen again and again. "No, Mama, let me 'lone!" And then a shriek, "Mama, come here NOW!"

There are days when the demands have been nonstop

since dawn. If I momentarily block out the din to reflect on my own beleaguered body and spirit, I become furious that my own needs have received no attention all morning. As long as I remained submerged in the swirling activity, numbly responding to all that was asked of me, I didn't flare up. Numbness was my defense against too many demands. But as soon as I noticed the unfairness of the situation, I gave warning that I had had enough. More was being asked of me than I could give. My ability to respond charitably to any further requests was absolutely depleted, so look out!

Anger at this juncture is a signal that one is being pressed beyond her capacity to cope. It's a danger sign, an indication that a person desperately needs time off.

Sometimes when I insist on a few moments alone, be it behind a locked bathroom door or elsewhere, I feel selfish and intolerant. Other times I melt with the awareness of my sons' charm and irresistible beauty; I wonder how I could come to resent them so terribly. *I love them.* Here is where the suffering lies. We love our children, but we do not love the taxing, monotonous routine of repetitious days.[3]

No mother can be there every single moment. No person can provide constant, complete satisfaction for a child. We wish we were capable of unconditional love, patience, and generosity. But such a mother is the stuff of a poetic fantasy that is doomed to failure. Love and anger coexist in each of us. Jealousy, rage, depression, confusion, and guilt may not be "mothering emotions" but they are normally present in all mothers. The question isn't, what is wrong with me for having these emotions, but how can I handle them constructively? We are not responsible to be everyone's dream mother or super mom.

Women differ from one another as much as men do. We

are born with every kind of human temperament. But strangely enough, this culture has only one image of the "good mother." She is quietly strong, selflessly giving, undemanding, unambitious, receptive, and intelligent in a moderate, practical way. Even-tempered, she controls her emotions. She loves her children completely and wholeheartedly.[4] Try as we might, most of us don't make the grade.

There are plenty of unexamined assumptions about mothers afloat. Call it the "motherhood mystique." They include the notions (1) that all women have instincts that men do not, instincts which enable women to care for babies and young children; (2) that mothers are "naturally" accepting and giving, with great reservoirs of patience; (3) that motherhood brings complete fulfillment to a woman; and (4) that no woman is fulfilled without having a child.[5]

These assumptions are false. They create guilt in women who don't match the myth. Even if a mother's nurturing is partially instinctive, much experience is necessary to learn to nurture well. What's more, you can have one child or twenty and feel more like a shrew than a fulfilled woman. Not everyone is better or more humane for having had children. Some parents' experience leads predominantly to resentment and frustration. You can also be a fulfilled woman and never have a child. The false mystique of motherhood makes women expect the wrong things from their parenting experience.

"If someone ever says to me, 'Woman is at heart a mother,'" writes Kathryn Lindskoog, "I am going to answer, 'Which woman?' Just as women all have vocal chords but some cannot sing well, so all women have reproductive organs but some cannot mother well. We are not all gifted in the same ways. It's no use pretending otherwise."[6]

In addition to the fatigue, the aloneness, and the failure to attain to super-motherhood, mothers are hounded by a residue of guilt that clings to them with a vengeance. We imagine that babies are born to be peaceful, gurgling cherubs and that it is only bad mothering that makes them otherwise. When a baby cries in public, people look askance at the mother. If a child behaves badly, people sneer at the parent's ineptitude.

Many folks feel superior to a mere mother, and qualified to give her unsolicited advice. The pressure to produce perfectly behaved, charming, and precocious children is so great that it's fair to imagine that *all* mothers feel guilt at some point for having failed their children. If the child is in any way less than an outstanding individual, the mother receives a disproportionate amount of blame and reproach.

Many a woman's self-confidence is depleted by motherhood. Sooner or later the child disappoints her, perhaps frightens her with a slight sign of distorted development, or subtle hint of temperamental weakness. If the child poisons himself, punches his eye with a scissors, or spills boiling coffee on himself, where is the blame usually directed? Naturally, at the one most often in charge: the mother.

And we expected her to be perfect. We entrusted her with the ultimate responsibility. She made an all-too-human mistake, and then gets saddled with a bundle of guilt. She failed the next generation. She failed the human race. Where are the adulations now, the hurrahs for having had the courage to try the impossible in the first place? No, you won't hear praise for her courage in trying—just blame for having failed.

As a parent I have moments of intense disquiet. A churning inner anxiety sets me down on occasion to reflect on this enormous trust. Some days I feel like a great, incredible mother capable of calling forth creativity, kindness, and cooperation from my two. On other days I drop into bed with a throbbing sense of failure, afraid that my best efforts will turn sour and my sons will grow to be warped, emotionally twisted adults.

My toddler varied so much from day to day. One day I'd think I couldn't abide one more whine, and my most gallant efforts to entertain him failed to quiet his incessant nagging. The next day was like a song. I'd merely suggest a play activity and he would grab it and go with it for hours.

One day I'm grateful that my son is an irrepressible conversationalist. He wins friends easily at the new Sunday school or among the people at the neighboring restaurant table. The next day his gift feels like a liability as Gerald and I connive to speak even a word with our dinner guests while this same son so eloquently monopolizes the conversation. What was so repressive about that old dictum that children should be seen and not heard?

Surely parenting is as precarious as a high-wire act. If you lean too far toward permissiveness, you slip into disaster. If you lean toward authoritarian arm-twisting, everyone suffers.

Those of us who vowed never to repeat our parents' mistakes catch ourselves doing things just as they did. We may find, as young parents, that part of our anger and depression comes from memories of negative patterns of interaction that we learned from our homes. If we desire not to be like an alcoholic mother or an abusive father, but find ourselves trapped and cycling in those destructive patterns, our alarms should motivate us to seek professional help and break the chain of doom.

On becoming a parent I have found that those who fail in their responsibilities as parents have a new claim on my sympathies. I know all too well the taste of uncertainty. It is said that "to be a father rather than a son is to learn the inevitability of failure."[7]

Not until I became an uncertain, failing parent did I understand that my mother and father were only a woman and a man, who had among other accomplishments, raised eight children. I felt reconnected with the humanity that I share with my parents because I had become what they are. It was as though I were seeing them as complex, developing, uncertain persons in their own right for the first time, whereas I had seen them before as merely fulfilling their parental roles. After roughhousing on the floor with his dad one day, Joseph sat down at the table and sang smilingly from a favorite record, "Grown-ups are only big children."

I used to think parents pushed their own children toward birthing the next generation in order to perpetuate the family line, or because they are eager to become doting grandparents. However that may be, I now believe that parents long for their children to become parents so that they can finally be understood by their oft rebellious offspring. Those who have gone before seem to sense some historic justice when we youngsters learn to suffer, to give up our irresponsible childishness, to compromise because of another's needs. Is it too much to hope that when children have grown beyond their arrogant youth to understand their own limitations as new parents, they may turn to extend tolerance, comfort, and forgiveness to their own parents?

Timothy responded to my self-directed burst of anger one

day with, "What's the matter, Mommy? Don't worry,
Mommy." Barely two, he is a long way from parenthood,
but as I acknowledged his comfort I hoped that a seed of
compassion would survive bumpy adolescence and young
adulthood. One day he might again lovingly say, "Don't
worry, Mom. You did the best you could. Thanks."

Shortly before our wedding I heard of a family with
severe problems in mutual understanding. "That's so unnecessary," I said callously. "If they had only done this and
that differently they wouldn't have so many difficulties."
After my wedding and especially on becoming a mother, I
remembered my words with profound embarrassment.

There are seminars and popular bandwagons claiming
that if parents just have the right chain of command, or
claim the right Bible promises, or implement the stan-
dardized model of Christian parenthood, God will not let
their children depart from the faith.

The Bible doesn't present such a simplistic view of life,
however. We humans are complex, free-willed creatures
made in the image of God. The effects of sin and unseen
spiritual forces, the lure of the predominant culture, and the
fallenness of human nature all make simplistic answers
inadequate. These factors affect even strong Christian
homes.

We are responsible for training our children with the best
of our hearts and minds, but mistakes, unforeseen traumas,
and a child's free choice may bring disappointing results.
That is part of life. It is wise to be honest in admitting that
all will likely not turn out as we hope, and be open to learn
from surprises, both pleasant and unpleasant. If parents can
freely confess their capacity to err, accept God's healing
grace, and move on in ministry to others, they need not live

nervously under the illusion that there is a foolproof formula for producing perfect progeny.

Rare is the parent who is brash enough to boast, "I've done a splendid job in raising my children." When our children even remotely resemble what we hoped and prayed they would become it is a miracle of grace. Christ's strength is made perfect in our weakness, not our success. Parents struggling with guilt and self-condemnation do not need simplistic platitudes. They need friends who will "weep with those who weep."

All parents weep at one time or another because more is needed from them than they can give. "The loveliest baby on earth is a summons to suffering by the fifteenth year, often long before," writes Lewis Smedes. "When you conceive a child, you covenant to suffer."[8]

When things become difficult, we may doubt our decision to parent. We feel unsure, sinful, or just plain stupid. How then can we cope with our limitations? Let's consider three approaches:

(1) *Relax*. I have discovered that I cope better if I can relax and accept less rigorous standards for myself. I am fallible and need to accept it. I should be consistent in disciplining my sons, but I have my inconsistent moments. I will never match the mother celebrated on a sacred pedestal at Mother's Day. I am not completely selfless. I get angry, yell, and sulk. My family isn't always happy.

Being a mother has forced me to relinquish some of my egotism. I am a becomer, a "kid under construction," just a few years ahead of my own children. Some parents do better than others, but each of us is growing; as we gain confidence, parenting becomes more fun. I feel I've increased in maturity with each child. With our second son I felt more comfortable as a mother, knowing that it's okay to blow it sometimes. He will survive. He can forgive and bless me with forgetfulness. He will be wiser for knowing that parents also have needs, rights, and thresholds of tolerance.

Life with children is an exciting adventure, the more so because there is little certainty in it, other than our all too uncertain humanity. The sooner we are humble enough to admit that it's all right to struggle, to doubt, to fail, the sooner we can relax and enjoy the adventure. Being humble means sharing my brokenness to help others become comfortable with who and what they are. We can "weep with those who weep" when we ourselves know repentance and Jesus' forgiveness.

(2) *Be flexible.* Children have a marvelous penchant for squelching schedules. If you aren't flexible before you have children, you will flex afterward, or crack up. Your most carefully laid plans will likely fall apart at the last minute. To accept the change usually takes less time and energy than does exploding. Laughter in such a moment does wonders. I recall one such occasion when Gerald and I grew more and more irritated and snappy, resenting every interruption and delay until the whole scenario looked so ludicrous that we broke into gales of laughter, tabled our plans, and cracked jokes about our ridiculous situation. Transforming the absurd into the comic brings a healthy balm to our labored, overscheduled lifestyle.

Our little ones are too often being rushed and shoved along—hurry here, hurry there—when they just want to dawdle and delay. In this stage of parenting it is imperative to slow down and simplify our life for their sake. The children's diversionary tactics may be a sign that our agenda has been imposed on them inappropriately. When we are free to sit with them, hold them, read to them, and dangle our toes in the pond with them, their stalling won't matter.

We always arrange time for what we truly consider important. When our children are small, lolling along with them at their pace is truly important. It is said that children get in the way, but where are we going? Perhaps by going a few paces in our child's direction we'll arrive where we ought to be.

As the Shaker song put it:

'Tis the gift to be simple,
'Tis the gift to be free,
'Tis the gift to come down where we ought to be,
And when we find ourselves in the place just right,
'Twill be in the valley of love and delight.[9]

I like to think our home is that "valley," where we have all taken a break from the flurry to frolic for a season with our children while they are little.

If only we are not in too great a hurry to arrive at mastery all at once, we can be wife, mother, musician, poet, naturalist, writer—growing and inquiring along with our children. The mother who does best at home is not Supermom, but the flexible woman who says, "Well, if it doesn't get done today, maybe tomorrow." If we willingly slow down and relax about the fragmentation of these years, our life will be blessed and hopefully give blessing.[10]

Luxurious houses, fine clothes, and expensive cars are hardly in tune with the child among us. We can't afford to compare ourselves with the wrinkle-free model women of the jet set. The women who impress me most are those who have embraced change and disappointment and soared to new heights because of them.

As I made room for a child's nonstop demands, more space opened for others to move into my life. Since I interrupted my work countless times for a youngster, why not just as easily drop it for a cup of coffee with an unannounced visitor? With little ones underfoot, I soon discovered that hospitality cannot include elaborate productions. I have decided rather to simplify my menu and do the bare minimum essential for entertaining. Then I can relax and enjoy the company. The value of being hospitable isn't in the style, but in the genuine friendship shared with others.

(3) *Spend time alone.* A lovely poem by Emily Dickinson describes, I think, the secret of surviving motherhood:

> Have you got a brook in your little heart,
> Where bashful flowers blow,
> And blushing birds go down to drink,
> And shadows tremble so?
>
> And nobody knows, so still it flows,
> That any brook is there;
> And yet your little draught of life
> Is daily drunken there.[11]

There should be a sacred interlude for every mother within the pattern of her day, when she can retire into her own inner world and tend to some of her own needs. Every parent needs time alone to maintain that center of being. Unless we take time out to nourish our own spirit, our inner brook will dry up. We will find ourselves parched and incapacitated.

A woman who respects herself will teach others around her to respect her need for quiet and space. Her children can, in turn, learn from her example to appreciate creative silence, and to find their own inner brook.

When I felt most overwhelmed by my "close encounter with toddling beings," I determined to maintain a discipline of daily reading and writing, scant though it would have to be. *I* need nurture if I'm going to nurture. Some of the most nurturing times for me are playing the piano, listening to Beethoven, going for a walk, writing in my journal, or just sitting quietly with *no distractions*. A good time no longer means going to a restaurant or a movie. A good time now means absolute quiet. To be alone is the most exciting diversion I know, and the most essential! I am much more able to give love after just fifteen minutes of peace.

Our children will eventually grow up and leave us. We need selves of our own to return to then. If we do not now hang on to a life of our own, standing alone and apart on occasion, we may well find that we've become empty dry shells which will blow away after we can no longer cling to our children for our identity.

The healthiest thing a young mother can say is, "In the midst of all my giving, there are certain things I will not give up. Time alone is one of those things." Women need to know themselves as creative persons, as friends, as partners, distinct from their responsibilities as mothers.

Some mothers might need jobs outside the home to maintain their equilibrium, or a daily walk by the lake, or an hour a day for reading. More rest might be all the cure some need in order to cope.

One morning I noticed that my 18-year-old Swiss watch had lost 60 minutes. Our only clock went on the blink that same morning, and Gerald's digital watch suddenly started over (0000) at 7:10 a.m. It seemed that someone was trying to stop time for us. What a priceless gift that would be, I thought—to rest, finally catch up, and move on refreshed.

In *Mister God This Is Anna,* six-year-old Anna asked, "Why did Mister God rest on the seventh day?"

"I suppose he was a bit flaked out after six days' hard work," replied 19-year-old Fynn.

"He wasn't tired," objected Anna.

"Wasn't he?"

"No—he made rest. Yes, that's the biggest miracle. Rest is," Anna continued. "When he was finished making all the things, Mister God had undone all the muddle. Then you can rest, so that's why rest is the very, very biggest miracle of all."[12]

As a mother too often caught in the muddle, I resonate completely with Anna's assertion. God *made rest.* Rest is the greatest miracle imaginable in our chaotic world! It's profoundly unjust if a woman who makes rest for her family cannot herself find adequate time to be alone to hear God's still small voice. Fathers, friends, uncles, aunts, grandparents—hear, hear! Your offer to entertain the baby even for an hour is a priceless gift of mercy! Those who took my child for a walk or played with him for an evening, restored my soul.

And so we move on. Parenthood's lesson in tolerance brings us the fruits of compassion and wisdom. As we understand our own humanity, we judge others less for theirs. As we watch a baby become a child and then an adult we become wise to the infinite complexity of human nature. And there is something else to be gained as well. It is what Anne Morrow Lindbergh calls a "timeless inner strength."[13] It is a powerful resilience that results from meeting our children's demands day after day, which forces us to discover secret wellsprings of strength within our being.

When we become parents we appreciate in a new way the

"cycles of eternity." The newborn is a miracle as fresh as if a birth had never occurred before in human history. The baby grows into a child, then an adult, leaves home, marries, and gives birth—and a new springtime has come before anyone realized the old one had passed. The parents, now grandparents, "rediscover the meaning of their own spring." They find it is not diminished because it has passed, but enriched because it has been repeated. This is the great gift of the spirituality of the family and the covenant of parenthood in particular: a direct participation in the "cycles of eternity" and the chance to see within the sharing of human love the working of a greater Love.[14]

Sometimes after dark, as I stand beside the beds of my sleeping children, my heart throbs with painful joy. My irritation, exasperation, impatience, and the busyness of the day past seem crass beside their beautiful, cherubic, and trusting faces. Now asleep, they are the picture of peace. Would that as their rambunctious bodies hurtle through my day I could embrace them as gifts to teach me, share life with me, remind me of my own beginnings and my approaching age. I look at my sons and pray that I can be a wise mother, and that they will become sturdy, compassionate men. It is a fragile process. There are scars and bruises. The way is long. Our efforts can be torn down by war, sickness, disaster, human failure. And yet we build that fragile beauty, hoping that resilience will accompany maturity, praying that our weakness will be made sufficient by God's grace.

9

Interdependence

All Fair in Work and Play

Father! father! where are you going?
O do not walk so fast.
Speak, father, speak to your little boy,
Or else I shall be lost.

The night was dark, no father was there;
The child was wet with dew;
The mire was deep, and the child did weep,
And away the vapour flew.

—*William Blake*[1]

It was Tuesday morning, my day for desk work and Gerald's day for child care and housework. I felt guilty sitting in quiet at my desk, behind a closed door, because I knew Gerald had a lot of his own work to do. My love for him made me want to facilitate his work rather than placing additional demands on him for child care. As I sat there musing, however, I heard the boys' happy voices chattering with their dad. Their delight in their father gave me a joy that ran deeper than my momentary guilt.

I felt a profound rightness about the arrangement. It was right to have some moments to myself to rejuvenate. My previous inclination was to give and give to my husband and sons until I came to resent their demands. Resentment and exhaustion had severely undermined my ability to relate re-demptively to them. Our solution was to structure our life so that there are spaces of time when I can wash my hands of family responsibilities, turn things over to Gerald, and look to my own needs for a few hours without distraction.

I listened to the male trio making plans to liberate our frisky pet mouse in a distant park. The boys were eager to show their dad how two-year-old Timothy braves the high twirl slide. I rejoiced. What a loss it would be for Gerald to miss out on such thrills, had he sold his soul to his graduate studies. If we believed the university to be the primary arena for him to prove his mettle, the boys would live with a father mostly absent from their daily lives. None of us would hear the elation of, "Daddy found a special little 'house' for our mouse," and "Daddy helped us build a BIG mountain of sand!" The rapport between a father and his children is priceless!

The impetus for more deliberate sharing of parental responsibilities between us came as I was able to articulate my desire and need to develop as a person in roles other than child-rearer. The more I had become submerged in the rounds of parental responsibilities, the more clearly I sensed the need to remove myself from those responsibilities in order to keep things in proper perspective. I wanted other adults and the father of my children to relieve my nonstop vigil. A mother's need for self-preservation provides the practical push for change in the traditional patterns.

The most persuasive feminist vision for us is one of mutuality—not a rigid egalitarian, 50/50 sameness, but a mutuality in which each of us is free to balance personal time-out and family responsibilities. Our commitment to partnership needed to be reevaluated after Joseph's birth. We found ourselves slipping into patterns in which Gerald's work had priority. I waited for a break until he gave it to me, but his work never seemed to reach a point of completion. The pressure would build up to intolerable levels within me.

"Why aren't your research and writing ever finished?" I chided. Only gradually did we begin to comprehend that his work by its very nature had no real closure. It was always open-ended. Unless we negotiated time off for me, I would continually dangle in the hope that my eternally studious husband would some day soon reach the end of inquiries. Instead, we began to structure our time-sharing differently; I could count on my own time, and Gerald usually managed to tailor his own projects accordingly.

I want to affirm those women who choose child-rearing and homemaking as their primary work for a season. The ideal of shared parenthood need not be for everyone. It should not be seen as just one more pressure on parents to perform, conform, or "get with it." Many of us women prefer to do the primary child care. We like it that way. That's fine.

But motherhood without choice, without time-outs, without support is a very quick road to losing control and destroying oneself (and one's children as well). The first step toward sanity is to acknowledge that normal human beings cannot usually perform well all the tasks dumped onto a mother's lap. If all the tasks are to be completed and children well-cared-for, other persons must be involved.

Was it ever normal or humane or Christian to isolate a woman in a suburban house with a tribe of youngsters while her husband bustles off to his job? For the beleaguered mother, a nuclear family is often lonely and debilitating. The husband and wife shared in making those babies. They can determine together to share more fairly the care of those little ones. Deliberate restructuring *can* bring the father back into family life.

I remember well how I repeatedly got up during the night in response to Timothy's demands to nurse. Rather than decreasing in frequency, they were increasing as he passed his first birthday. Night after night of interrupted sleep turned me into a miserable, distraught woman. After other tactics failed, I finally put down my foot and insisted that Gerald and I sleep on the floor in the living room overnight; I would be out of Timothy's sight, if not out of mind.

For many nights after our move, Gerald got up to reassure Timothy and offer him a drink from a bottle, while I snuggled contentedly under the covers. I regretted that Gerald's work and rest suffered, but I began to move toward a moderate restoration and a more acceptable nursing schedule. Thanks to Gerald's willingness to bear the brunt of a little boy's rage when mother didn't appear, we all found a more wholesome equilibrium.

Parenting stimulates people to mature. It is an important job for both men and women to learn to be nurturing, tender, patient, gentle, and playful. Maybe if "mothering" became "parenting" and fathers took on a fairer share of the responsibility, our children would receive more top-quality care. To persist in using "motherhood" instead of "parenting" means we continue to conjure up romanticized images of complete self-sacrifice. "Motherhood" shores up the myth that only women can do the important parts of child-rearing, and that only women should be entirely selfless while doing it. "Parenting" suggests an equal or cooperative relationship between mother and father in sensitively caring for the needs of the next generation.

The question of the quality of child care is the strongest argument in favor of shared parenting. Everyone benefits as mother and father share the load, *especially the children.* Many fathers stuck in the traditional patterns have deserted their children hourly and daily. Many children are virtually fatherless; some of this is due to homes broken under the strains, but in other cases it is simply because we have valued our jobs or our paychecks over our children.

Gerald and I are committed to the frequent, attentive presence of both mother and father in the lives of our children. It isn't fair to our children to pen them up with one beleaguered adult day after day. One person should not be expected to provide all a child's needs. It's a disadvantage when a child is limited to an exclusive and intense relationship with only one person.[2] If that one person is angry or tired, to whom can the child turn for reassurance? It seems unhealthy for an unformed little child to experience such a massive input from a single personality, especially if that one person is herself lonely and frustrated. The mother-child relationship is critically important. Without it children are in severe trouble. But a mother and child can suffer severely when their husband and father chooses to give priority to professional success, expecting his wife to pick up the family tab.

"As an advocate for babies," writes T. B. Brazelton, an authority on child development, "I know that the more pleasure parents can feel in their role, the better the baby will feel about him or herself."[3] Shared parenting manifoldly increases my ability to enjoy my children and my husband.

When Gerald takes the boys on an outing, prepared to handle diapers and bottles, I am awash in love for him. It is wonderful to sit down several times a week to a meal my husband has prepared, to listen to him crow, "I get real satisfaction out of putting on this show!" The soup is thicker, heartier, spicier than I normally make it; the cheese and pretzels are more artfully arranged. A simple delight. Child care and housework are still primarily mine because I've chosen to major on them in this particular phase of our pilgrimage. However, a structure for some shared parenting and clear delineation of household responsibilities has freed me to enjoy parenting rather than being destroyed by it. No husband can possibly overdo this cooperation; he has nothing to lose and everything to gain from increasing his wife's freedom to enjoy the parenting they share.

The roles available to women are changing in our society. More mothers are finding employment and other involvements outside the home than ever before. Whatever the reasons for these changes, it is not fair to make women take the rap for a lot of the other changes going on in the society at the same time. Some studies try to link increased violent child abuse to increased employment of women. Such simplistic pointing the finger of blame does nothing to solve anything.

The tradition of placing blame for trouble at home on the mothers is a very sore point! Where are the fathers? More than likely they have deserted their families, leaving mothers and children to struggle on their own. Since when is it solely a woman's responsibility to keep the family from falling apart? Why should only the female parent be forced to choose between personal goals and family well-being?

Some few of today's men are being liberated from the "male tenderness taboo" and joining in with responsibility for the care of children. Their masculinity is in no way compromised. Happy is the child whose father cares deeply enough to give up privilege and a hectic pursuit of success to play, work, and relax with his family. Happy is the child whose mother believes enough in herself to insist on creating livable space around her. Passivity, self-hatred, and low expectations in a mother become an oppressive inheritance, especially when passed on to daughters. A mother who knows her own unique worth as a gifted woman may communicate something to her daughter which is more precious than her full-time presence as mothering person would provide.

We have in this society overlooked the strong, natural desire of fathers to know their infants. We have neglected the critical function fathers play in enriching a baby's experience by providing a second caring adult. "We have gone from father as autocrat to father as nothing," laments Kathryn Lindskoog. "We need to find a Fatherhood of compassionate but firm discipline and moral fiber."[4]

Differences between father's and mother's style widen the child's perspective on the world. A father need not imitate the mothering function. Replication is not as enriching as complementarity of softness and toughness, nurturing and playful roughhousing. Roles can even be exchanged between father and mother if one is psychologically more suited to particular tasks than the other; the parental composite should preserve strength and gentleness, structure and freedom.

We need to look at arrangements where husband and

wife can cooperate both in outside occupations and home responsibilities. Developmental psychologist Brazelton views the increasing role for men in child-rearing as one of the most obvious and best trends in this generation.[5] We now have the opportunity to foster two successful roles for each parent: jobs and nurturing roles. As women take greater responsibility for the family's financial needs, husbands should be freer to relax their job demands and to better balance family and work obligations.

If a father can take out time to be the care-giver while a mother needs to be at work, both he and the child profit. Even if the father cares for the children for only a few hours, suggests Brazelton, the mother will feel less overextended and the father will gain enormously in his sense of self as a nurturing person.[6]

Times certainly are changing, and in some ways for the better. Ten years ago, the rising young executive with 2.4 children and a captive wife stood ready to go anywhere, anytime, for corporate success. "Now I rarely see that man," says Robert Booth, head of Corporate Recruiters, who scouts personnel for the country's top corporations. "The new executive draws the line at uprooting the family."[7]

In contrast with previous generations, young men are less obsessed with an image of masculinity as privilege. They accept as given what their fathers would not have dreamed of—the equal importance of women's goals. Many of them expect to share the breadwinning tasks with their wives, and they emphasize family life more than work.[8] Now that's progress!

More men are turning down overtime, transfers, and promotions in favor of more time at home and a more stable family life. They are making at least some gestures toward sharing the housework with their employed wives.[9] Whether fundamental, pervasive changes are really in the offing is not yet clear, but we have seen a glimmer of a more wholesome way of relating.

Let's look again at the contributions that a move toward more shared parenting can facilitate in our families. (1) The child will likely experience affectionate attachment to both parents and receive enrichment from the skills of both mother and father. (2) Neither parent will feel overly burdened with child care nor deprived of a vigorous relationship with the child. (3) The mother will be able to maintain outside contacts of an adult nature, and the father will gain skills in child care. (4) Each of the parents will compromise a bit because neither can do everything he or she would like.

Priority is given by all to family life. One caution: whether parenting is done in a traditional fashion or is shared on an egalitarian basis, there is no single perfect way. Each way has its essential difficulties. Each couple and family must freely find the style or compromise which serves each of its members best.

Many feminists speak of equality as synonymous with sameness in career development. For all I have just said about sharing job and child care, I want to affirm again that equality does not mean sameness.

Some marriages can function on traditional lines with a career for the man and homemaking for the woman, or vice versa. If both enjoy what they are doing, and each spouse feels whole, it can be a relationship of equality, one of mutual valuing and respect. Partners in a marriage can consider their roles equally important even if society rewards and regards them differently. If each partner feels able to be creative, to expand horizons, to fulfill priorities, to be what

God designed each to be, such a marriage *is a relationship based on equality!* Each of us deserves the opportunity to develop to our fullest potential, but this is not the same as climbing the professional ladder. Self-development may just as easily happen at home for the man or the woman, as out there somewhere.

The mutual relationship of love and respect that we strive for is one in which compromises are made on the basis of what is fair for each and best for our relationship and our family together. Parenting does not come naturally to the father or to the mother; it is part of a sanctification process, a process that forms us more fully into the image of our Maker. Both husband and wife are called to fulfill their ministries, sharing the gospel as they are able, as they are gifted. Each spouse is called to facilitate the other's best ability to minister. This is the biblical vision of mutuality.

Why am I emphasizing mutuality and shared parenting? Is it not obvious to everyone that husbands and wives are supposed to work together? Let's look more closely at why this is still such a critical issue. The power relationships that develop within the family are *the most basic* forms of oppression in our world. Ours is a society that condones a husband's right to treat his wife as he wishes. Yes, even our so-called modern society has not yet rid itself of the notion that a woman is the property of her man, required to submit to him and fulfill his every demand. Many women's bruised bodies and broken spirits give painful evidence that women are treated as property, as slaves condemned to dependence on their husbands.

Hierarchic legalism and repression of women find support in the pervasive assumption that female subordination was created by God. The husband's traditional "rule over his wife" fans the flames of male pride, self-righteousness, and abusive behavior. This pattern of male dominance and female inferiority is a crass distortion of God's original creation, which was complementary: "in the image of God ... male and female he created them."

Genesis 1 and 2 show male and female as copartners in their responsibilities for tending and taming the earth. Sin has clearly corrupted the beauty of male/female distinctions. Sin has turned the very genius of God's diversified, complementary creation into a brittle system, stratifying people into oppressive ranks of superior and inferior power.

Patricia Gundry, in *Heirs Together*, describes in commonsense logic how this systematized oppression manages to obtain such a stranglehold on our relationships:

> The woman will more and more tend to rely upon her husband, be dependent upon him because of her many pregnancies and small children to care for, and as a result of her dependency, he will take advantage of her need and dominate her. I think it predicts the beginning of the true essence of worldliness: Those who are vulnerable look to the powerful for help, and the powerful exploit their power and rule over and mistreat the vulnerable. The process becomes complex and intertwines, extending itself geometrically until it has permeated all relationships.[10]

Right here within the family context is the key choice between redemptive or oppressive ways of relating. Unless a husband can refrain from taking advantage of his wife (weakened in childbirth and child care), he becomes an exploiter, an oppressor. Unless he becomes vulnerable and weak himself in caring for his wife and children, he is potentially a violent tyrant. This is the essence of worldliness and godlessness, because a man of such insensitivity sacrifices loving human relationships in his quest for dominance and power.

The church has unfortunately contributed to unredemptive ways of relating by putting more emphasis on "Wives, submit to your husbands" than on "Husbands, love your wives as your own bodies." The church's preoccupation with the headship of the husband is lopsided and distorted. It reflects more the prejudices of our time than the biblical ideal. Since the wife is most often in the vulnerable position, it behooves every husband and father to offer himself as helper, care giver, and servant, to give himself to his wife as Christ gave himself to the church.

It is pathetic and ironic that the very passage which calls on husbands to sacrifice themselves for their wives has been misconstrued by many Christians as giving license to a husband to use his wife's service to enhance his own privilege. It is the way of the world to assume that the stronger shall rule the weaker. The truly Christian way of relationships calls everyone into the service of everyone else, and the strong especially must serve the weaker.[11] Contrary to what you might conclude from popular religious broadcasts today, it is not a hierarchical structure that makes a family Christian. It is rather an entirely new way of relating to each other in mutual submission.

Jesus introduced a radically new understanding of power, authority, and servanthood. He turned patriarchal paternalism absolutely upside down. Whenever one group is lifted above another, he asserted in his words and actions, there is a power at work that is *antithetical* to the gospel:

> You know that those who are regarded as rulers of the Gentiles lord it over them, and their high officials exercise authority over them. Not so with you. Instead, whoever

wants to become great among you must be your servant, and whoever wants to be first must be slave of all. Mark 10:42-44.

Jesus consistently defied structures that would deny women their full humanity. He dealt directly with women, not just through their husbands and fathers. By commending the touch of an "unclean" woman, he defied the religious structure; by encouraging the theological understanding of Mary and Martha, he defied the educational structure; by demanding a lasting commitment of both partners in marriage, he defied the legal structures.[12] Jesus' response to these oppressive institutions was not a kindly paternalism, but a clarion call to change the fundamental distortions of patriarchy.

Jesus is a role model for quality parenting. If you equate nurture and compassion with the mothering role, then Jesus too was a mothering person. Jesus called males and females to parent each other in this sense: we are compelled to serve one another, becoming the least among us, so that others may be enhanced.

Jesus was no macho "man's man." We don't see him swaggering and flexing muscles to prove his masculinity. He did not shrink from showing tender affection to men, women, and children. He was gentle but powerful, meek but incredibly brave. He wept in public. He was resolute and bold when facing down the forces of evil. He minced no words in demanding justice and righteousness. Jesus was (and is) the model of perfectly integrated personhood.

By choosing to become a servant, Jesus brings dignity to the role of the lowly servant. We need to remind ourselves that Christ was not a victim. He said to his disciples, "No one takes [my life] from me, but I lay it down of my own accord. I have authority to lay it down and authority to take it up again" (John 10:18).

Virginia Ramey Mollenkott suggests that God was incarnated in a free male, neither a slave nor a woman, because Jesus came to teach us that the proper use of power is to use it on behalf of those who have no power. The Messiah, the Sent-One, had to be *free* in a slave-owning society, and *male* in a sexist society. He had to possess power in order to demonstrate its proper use. "Christ as self-giver was held up as a model for those persons who *had power to give up,* not to those who had no power in the first place."[13]

Jesus chose servanthood. He did not meet life as a trampled, defeated doormat. He plunged aggressively, with purpose and passion, into his society. He shared the joys and sufferings of others, bringing hope, transformation, and resurrection power.

The goal of biblical feminism is for women and men to achieve a sense of their autonomy under God, of inner and outer freedom, and of power to minister, so that they can in turn *choose* Christlike servanthood. "Power" is a healthy and good word. We are empowered by the Spirit to heal, to nurture, to love, and to serve. Elisabeth Schüssler Fiorenza put it this way:

> Feminist spirituality proclaims wholeness, healing love and spiritual power not as hierarchical, as *power over*, but as *power for*, as enabling power.[14]

It is hard to be a servant and to be submissive when everyone treats you like a servant. Sometimes we have to say "no" to servile slavery, so that we can say "yes" with all our hearts to aggressive, courageous servanthood. The reason we can serve is because Jesus Christ first of all supremely served us. To be like him is to be a servant with dignity, worth, and enabling power.

And so it follows that our husbands, when they serve as Christ served the church, free us to serve because *they are servants first*. To serve one another in joyful submission is to fulfill the law of Christ. For the secular feminist movement, the goal is egalitarianism. For the biblical feminist, the objective is mutual submission.

As Christian feminists we seek freedom from servility; we seek the glorious liberty of the children of God. But we don't seek power to promote ourselves in the interest of selfish egos. We desire above all to use our liberty and power in order "to serve each other out of reverence to Christ."

The solution to a pro-male bias is not to replace it with a pro-female bias. God created male and female to live in harmony, not enmity. Men and women must work together in complementary relationships in order to discover the exquisite joy of God's original intention. [15]

Some in the secular feminist movement would have us believe that we have achieved victory when we see women functioning as men. Such a view, it seems to me, merely confirms traditional male superiority. It is no compliment to be told that I think like a man, or that I have the confidence of a man. A man is no standard for a woman. The best of femaleness is her standard.

We can discard out of hand a femininity that is coy, shallow—a spineless sham of the true goodness of womanhood. Womanly virtues include warmth, tenderness, and self-giving as well as strength and boldness. Femininity involves the forthright use of our hearts and minds, as well as our wombs.

Some folks go to great lengths emphasizing the difference

between men and women, so as to confine them to their proper roles and functions. Others stress the many similarities. Dr. Willard Krabill writes:

> We have yet to fully understand biologically, developmentally, physiologically how alike we are. And where we are not alike, we are either equal or complementary. There should be no room for a double standard in Christian circles. God created us sexual, male and female, each unable to exist without the other.[16]

I don't doubt that there are basic differences between men and women. I find those differences reason for celebration. Diversity is enlivening, creative. Yet, as C. S. Lewis remarked, it is the most purely feminine women and the most purely masculine men who are the most dull.[17] The most fascinating men are those who are sensitive, tender, and playful, as well as brave and strong. There is a special kind of virility in a man who comforts as well as confronts. A man secure in his masculinity need not flaunt his macho prowess.

The most intriguing women are those who are articulate and valiant, as well as gentle, considerate, and fun to be with. The great persons among us are those who, like Christ, manage to integrate the best of human qualities.

Those of us who tend to be nurturing, feeling people have a responsibility to develop the part of us that is rational and thoughtful, and vice versa, all in an effort to become more whole. We are not urged in the Bible to be masculine, or feminine, but to be like Christ. We are called to mature personhood in Jesus, "until we all reach unity in the faith and in the knowledge of the Son of God and become mature, attaining to the whole measure of the fullness of Christ" (Ephesians 4:13).

The very fact of our complementary differences poses the strongest argument for opening all vocations to both men and women. Since a man can give something to children that a woman perhaps cannot, and a woman can add a special quality to a work team that a man perhaps cannot, we do ourselves an enormous favor to integrate men and women into all walks of life. In becoming whole, integrated people, we do not blot out our distinctions. No, we simply value our differences rather than using them as excuses for division or oppression.

The traditional marriage pattern of dominance and subservience is unbiblical. Interdependence in marriage can be a life-affirming and growing relationship. There are times when I give in to my husband's wishes and put aside my own interests, in order to encourage and build him up. There are also times when he lays aside his personal preferences to assist me. Many times we both make sacrifices so that our children's needs can be met. A marriage where tasks are divided according to interests and abilities rather than according to fixed and rigid roles is deeply fulfilling.

Abraham Maslow writes that one of the characteristics of loving, mature couples is that they do not make sharp differentiations between the roles and personalities of the two sexes.[18] Certainly no marriage can be happy when the wife domineers and selfishly puts her husband down. Neither is a marriage very upbuilding when a wife must be weak and demurring so that a husband can feel strong and on top of things. The most satisfying relationships are those where the "head of the house" isn't at issue, because each cares first for the other's happiness. The traditional pattern of patriarchal headship and passive submission is an immature pattern for those who seek an intimacy based on parent-child needs for each other. Much more fulfilling intimacy can be shared in an adult-adult relationship where two autonomous, unique persons nurture and build each other up.

Parenting is a team effort. Having children can bring partners closer together if parenthood is shared between mother and father. An affectionate and cooperative relationship between parents creates a wholesome environment for children. Our world is awash with destructive stereotypes of men and women which our children absorb like sponges. One day I overheard four-year-old Joseph and a girl friend conversing:

"Daddies are wild," declared one. "They have hammers and swords. Mamas only take care of babies."

(My heart sank. Was that the message getting through the barrage of contemporary male-female messages?) But then the conversation continued.

"Let's take turns. You stay home with the baby." The girl then roared off in her car.

"Rock-a-bye, baby," sang Joseph, and then he quipped, "It's your turn to make supper."

Another day Joseph came home and announced: "There was a man teacher today. That's unusual. And a woman drove the bus. Isn't that funny?"

Strange, maybe, but just fine! Would that my son could more often see strong men caring for little children, and capable women driving buses.

I'm thrilled to see a "maternal instinct" in my husband. He's not always as understanding as I think he should be, but then neither am I always gifted with boundless patience and sensitivity. At times he's unsure and unskilled in caring for the children, resisting greater responsibility for their care. Sometimes I resent it that he isn't as intimately acquainted with the myriad minutiae that make up our sons' lives. Yet I dare not ignore how *persistent* he is in caring for me, loving our children, and *learning* to nurture all of us with increasing sensitivity. New fathers have few models in this role!

A young mother, pregnant with her second child, asked me one morning how I like having two children. I answered that there are days when I am exasperated and overspent, but that overall I enjoy mothering two, because my husband and I have structured things so that I have time off. She looked surprised. "Many others say it's *so* hard!" she lamented.

The more often we see women isolated for long days with demanding youngsters, women who are fighting for their own survival and sanity, women who are burdened with unfair child care arrangements, the more we must cry out to husbands and fathers to be men of such Christlike stature that they will stoop to wash the feet of their wives and children. We need men of such brave fortitude that they will change their baby's smelly diapers and launder the mounds of soiled apparel. We need men of such generous godliness that they will share the yoke of child care and hold up their partner's arms day in and day out. Their wives and their children will forever honor and love them.

10

Solidarity

Acquainted with Grief

But often, in the world's most crowded streets,
But often, in the din of strife,
There rises an unspeakable desire
After the knowledge of our buried life;
A thirst to spend our fire and restless force
In tracking out our true, original course;
A longing to inquire
Into the mystery of this heart which beats
So wild, so deep in us—to know
Whence our lives come and where they go.
                        —*Matthew Arnold*[1]

Being a mother radicalized my outlook on life. I sensed what it is to be undervalued, discriminated against, disregarded. As part of a "class" that is not highly respected, I have learned to identify in a small way with women who are forced to question their self-worth by the oppressive policies and attitudes of those in power.

I grieved about my lowly status until I chose to embrace motherhood as a profoundly worthy vocation.

What can be done to protect, enhance, and enliven women who are mothers? Why has so little attention until recently been paid to the mother as a human being? It has been supposed that her function is simply to care for her child. Whether or not she can do it is beside the point. She *must* do it or reap condemnation from her society. How she feels and what she thinks have been deemed irrelevant.

Spending day after day with children has a demoralizing effect on anyone's self-concept. What can society and the church do, I wonder, to free women to enjoy their years of mothering? The gospel is not a negative dictum ordering women to shut up and keep their place at home. The gospel is compassionate good news reaching out to mothers who suffer under unbearable burdens, offering hope and relief.

Any dogma preaching that woman's place is strictly at home and that she must be satisfied there only increases her sense of powerlessness and loneliness. Unfortunately the church has too often overreacted to feminist positions and taken a defensive posture. Fear of extremes in the women's movement has led some religious leaders to push women back into a more narrow, subordinate sphere. They stress the few biblical passages with repressive imagery and ignore the pervasive liberating theology of human unity in the Spirit of God.[2]

It is tragic that the churches have so often protected a status quo of powerful males and passive females, rather than forging out in front of liberation movements to proclaim an even more radical truth: the gospel of love impels all men and women to serve each other and their children in humility.

The nurturing and caring that mothers do is infinitely worthwhile, but *particularly* evident as such when it is *chosen* by women who know themselves to be intelligent, capable, creative equal partners—not an inferior class of persons. Laws, church dogma, and societal structures that keep women down also devalue the nurture and care that are necessary for the survival of the human race!

As a *Christian* feminist, one can be critical of certain extremes within the women's movement. However, the fundamental feminist ideal of basic fairness toward men and women in the marketplace, in the law court, and at home is entirely consistent with Christian faith. Some feminist rhetoric has been directed against motherhood, and yet the movement as a whole has made great strides in restoring legal rights to women, and in encouraging women to be more responsible for their own gifts and development.

The women's movement has emphasized the truth that women are people in the first place, and then (some of them) also homemakers and mothers. Even while strongly supporting career lifestyles, the movement has also created a climate in which women can *choose* to stay at home. A woman today can claim motherhood as a highly worthwhile vocation and be proud of her work at home.

Many women now have the freedom to obtain an education, to marry or not to marry, to decide on the number of children, to enter a profession or to stay at home. They can share their gifts creatively, acting and thinking in ways that had hardly been possible before. Some are stymied by all the choices; they long for the good old days of more limited possibilities. Others are tempted to try too much in a vain effort at being Superwoman. However, if we can resist the temptation to measure our worth in salaries, we have received a chance to choose with new fervor an invaluable people-building vocation: motherhood.

The *Dictionary of Occupational Titles* more than a decade ago defined some 22,000 occupations on a "skill scale," from a high of one to a low of 887. How do mothers stack up against hotel clerks, for example, who rate 368? Homemakers, foster mothers, child care attendants, and nursery schoolteachers are all ranked at 878![3] That's about as low as you can get! The U.S. Labor Department apparently doesn't think much of mothers *or* children. The women's movement has brought much pressure for change on such twisted notions of skill and value. Thanks to their prophetic role in our society, parental skills are more highly esteemed today than a decade ago. The Labor Department's ranking scale just shows us how far we've had to come. The uphill climb stretches far into the distance.

Lawyers are currently struggling to assess the monetary value of a homemaker's work. When you calculate the cost of replacing this work by using professional services, figures soon run to tens of thousands of dollars annually. This can no longer be taken for granted. The terms of these valuations are hotly debated, but assigning concrete monetary values to the actual work is forcing all of us to reassess the homemaker's contribution.

More and more husbands are awakening to the realization that they could not afford to pay for what their wives have provided on an unpaid basis. It's crass to think that the real worth of a mother's work could be measured or even compensated in money, but I do delight in watching the dollar amounts soar into the hundreds of thousands of dollars as lawyers and clients argue about it.

There are further reasons for my feminism. I find biblical

feminism profoundly subversive, in a good not-of-this-world sense. John Alexander of *The Other Side* magazine observes that there are thousands of kinds of feminism, and not all kinds are equally subversive. One crucial division within feminism is between those who want women to make it into the system and those who want men and women to be free from it. The continuum stretches from those who want a woman to be president of Exxon to those who want men not to need to be president of Exxon.[4] If it be subversion to undermine the materialist, success-oriented value structure on which our society is built, in favor of Christ-centered values of loving service, then we need more subversives. When women cry out for justice, they join Jesus. When they oppose the selfishness of the male-dominated American success ethic, they do an essentially prophetic act.

One way to raise the status of child care, homemaking, and community volunteer work to the higher level of value they deserve is to have men do those tasks more often. When people with power and social prestige work at a task it has the effect of raising the valuation of that task. "Women's work" will never have the respect it deserves until it becomes women's and men's work.[5] Then we can honestly say that this is a family-oriented society and that we truly value and love our children.

The women's movement deserves credit for alerting us to the fact that women are earning only 59¢ for every dollar men earn in comparable work; minority women earn significantly less. Women are concentrated in the low-paying and nonpaying jobs. We are seeing an increasing feminization of poverty built on the double reality that women are poorly paid on the job, and more and more of them are the sole providers for their households. More men are lost to the narcissism of the prevailing culture; more women are abandoned to poverty. Too many women are forced to carry both roles: breadwinner and primary care-giver for children.[6]

Millions of American women are trying to survive on a fraction of the income and benefits normally enjoyed by men. Most mothers work because of economic necessity. More than two thirds of all working women are the sole providers for themselves and their children or are married to men who earn under $15,000 a year. Nineteen percent of American families are headed by women (15 percent of white families, 46 percent of black families) and 20 percent of America's children live with their mothers only.[7]

Raising children alone is an expensive, lonely, and debilitating job. "Welfare mothers" are stigmatized in our culture for "wasting" public funds. Selma Fraiberg writes sharply in their defense:

> In my own large experience with "welfare mothers" it is the rare woman who fits any of these stereotypes. . . . What we see among the "welfare mothers" are large numbers of women who are willing, and able, to make extraordinary personal sacrifices for their children, who show devotion and love for their children. . . . We see in them hopes and daydreams for their babies and young children which distinguish them in no way from economically advantaged parents. . . . When we visit them in their bleak and horrible apartments, see them wrestle with the blind bureaucracy that issues the relief check (not always on time), witness a meal that leaves every child hungry and ill-nourished, sit with them for hours in clinics where they and their children are ill-served and degraded, we can only ask ourselves how they have found resources within themselves to meet each day.[8]

Thank God that feminism is critiquing some of this social injustice and bringing some political muscle to enacting equal pay for equal work laws, fairer hiring practices, better working conditions, fairer medical and social security benefits, and reduction of sexual harassment in the workplace. The Older Women's League in a catchy ad notes: "For men, they created retirement plans, medical benefits, profit sharing, and gold watches. For women, they created Mother's Day." Feminists will take fair play and fair work any day over Mother's Day.

If we are genuinely concerned for mothers, one concrete thing we can do is to grant women full equality under the law. We can at least make sure that the law does not allow husbands disproportionate advantage in property rights, inheritance laws, and domicile laws. Although many married women enjoy a comfortable life, it is due to the kindness and generosity of a husband who wants it that way and earns enough money to make it a reality. It is certainly not, at present, a result of legal obligations.[9]

Since the homemaker is exceptionally vulnerable without income of her own and is entirely dependent on another person for her support, laws which give unfair power to the husband further undermine her position. A woman who is abandoned in divorce after working as a homemaker ends up with no income of her own and often with no skills or job experience with which to seek employment. She is usually hurt the most.[10] Only one third of divorced women with children receive child-support payments, and following a divorce the standard of living of most women *decreases by 73 percent*. The standard of living of men generally increases by 42 percent.[11]

Laws unfairly weighted in a husband's favor reflect a

deeper underlying cultural disregard for the value of the homemaker role. The homemaker's nonmonetary contribution to the family's welfare should be recognized in the family laws of every state in the country as being of equal value to that of the wage earner.[12]

Many women now suffering abuse from their husbands began marriage in an "appropriately" dependent role. The husband controls the money, the car, the decisions about job and housing; eventually he controls almost every aspect of his wife's behavior, perhaps forbidding her to see friends or to go out alone. The husband's demands and possessive behavior sometimes turns to beatings and other violent forms of abuse. Abused wives who have for years abdicated their own ability to make decisions are often slow to go for help. Many of them feel trapped in their abusive marriage situations by the needs of their children, by their lack of access to family finances, and by a debilitating dependence on their husbands.

Women sometimes try to keep the family together for the sake of the children, but the psychological damage and the toll of fear are so great that the abusive violence may finally lead the mother to remove the children and herself in the hope that the cycle of violence can somehow be broken.

A woman who makes such a decision is at a severe disadvantage. She is the spouse with no money and with the children. He has the money and no children. She cannot leave without money and transportation and housing, and yet she cannot qualify for welfare money until she leaves and establishes a new address. She cannot get a job without first finding somewhere to put her children. Even in such a no-win situation, some women summon enough courage to move out anyway. Of those who try, many are forced to go back by pressures too great to overcome. This makes it all the more unlikely that the cycle of violence can be broken in our generation.[13] Thanks to the women's movement, the number of shelters for abused women has grown in recent years, giving women and children the space and protection they need to establish themselves in a new life.

Various writings in the women's movement have made it abundantly clear that the legal status of the homemaker is insecure under existing legislation. Even more research has shown the multitudinous difficulties that confront a woman who wants to combine motherhood and a career. The option often suggested within the movement is to avoid career dilemmas by remaining childless. Society is not giving women much help or credit for trying to manage both job and children at the same time. Knowing how difficult it is to be full-fledged professionals and adequate mothers simultaneously, feminists are often choosing childlessness as the solution.

Perhaps there is another way. It would involve some extensive changes, but women could refuse to accept the painful choice between children and career by insisting on a society and employment options that make it easier to combine them. Both parents should have time for meaningful work and meaningful parenting, too. Businesses and companies need to move toward shorter, more flexible work shifts so that both father and mother can get off work or decrease their work loads to care for their family, especially in the critical early years. Part-time work now is disadvantaged (no pension benefits, seniority not acknowledged, no opportunity for advancement), but this would change if most workers were not chained to the 40-hour week.

Employers should be obligated to give maternity and

paternity leaves, permitting parents to share child care responsibilities. Businesses could provide child care facilities on their premises, allowing parents to take lunch and coffee breaks with their young children.

The first years of a child's life are precious and extremely critical. The mother who chooses to devote her energies to her children should receive society's best legal protection, practical financial support, and honorable mention for building up the fundamental unit of society, the family. If more men and women working in paid employment would insist that their employers recognize and support their family responsibilities, society just might begin to move toward more humane work situations for all workers.

The assumption now is that work and motherhood are antagonistic kinds of activity. Employment has been seen as a rejection of children and the maternal role. But the opposite is often true. Good workers make good mothers, and good mothers make good workers. In fact, if a woman shows a healthy amount of interest in her work, whatever it is, the prognosis is better for her enjoyment of motherhood.[14] A mature adult, male or female, values good work and also loves children.

A year ago we were moving to a more spacious apartment. Among our newly acquired furnishings was an old desk handed down from Grandpa Kraybill. I laid claim to it on first sight. Gerald preferred the new standard office desk we had purchased. For too many years since the boys were born, with characteristic deference I had allowed Gerald to have primary use of our only desk. His work usually involved more time there than mine, so I would set up shop on the kitchen table, and then dismantle my work when dinnertime arrived.

As we acknowledged my need for more private space and time, "mom's desk" found its special place in our new home. And what a boon Grandpa's beautiful wooden workplace was to my spirits.

For me to live without writing things down has always been confusing. I need time to work at writing, to reflect, to be creative. Other women need time to work at their teaching, art, organizing, administering, hospitality. Much has been written on the drawbacks of employment for mothers outside the home. Many children today are indeed neglected because both mother and father are absorbed in their work to such an extent that children's needs are not adequately cared for. Yet I believe it is beneficial for children when mother and father do have time to work at things other than child care, activities that bring them satisfaction and self-esteem in other ways.

Studies show that the most depressed women are those at home who wish they could be at work, and the least depressed are those who work and like it.[15]

Whole families suffer when their mother (wife) is unhappy and unfulfilled. Women who consider themselves martyrs obliged to sacrifice everything for their husbands and children are denying their families the joy of knowing a richly fulfilled woman. A child needs someone who is actively engaged in meaningful ways with the world around her, more than someone who is totally absorbed in child care and withering away in housework.

It is not proof of love to spend every minute of the day with another person, claims child psychologist Bruno Bettelheim.[16] Women who may not desire to work at any large project or paid job can and should at least read, sing hymns, cultivate flowers, or memorize poetry and Scripture.

Chosen, enjoyable work and maternal aspirations are entirely compatible.

Women who have pursued their own development, who are motivated to work and share their talents, who feel good about themselves as whole, well-rounded individuals—these women make good mothers. Feminists are right to urge women to expand their interests early in life lest they carry an unhealthy dependency and low self-image into their marriage and parenthood.

A woman who has proven to herself that she can handle difficult tasks and job opportunities will bring a more confident attitude and better-developed skills into mothering. Her husband and children benefit immeasurably from a wife and mother who knows where she is going in life and has a sense of being faithful to God's unique plan for her.

For some women, myself included, the best solution has been to work at home. Free-lance writers, copy editors, music teachers, and artists are in many cases managing to integrate work and child care on the home front. Old and new cottage industries are in fact thriving. At least five million workers now earn money while staying right at home; projections are that the number and variety of such jobs could easily double by 1990. Telecommuting (information processing via telephone hookup between a home terminal and a company computer) has opened a new range of possibilities for working at home in a wide variety of professional careers. One estimate suggests that half of the work force could eventually do telecommuting from their own homes!

Workers in many other fields are also attempting to change the pattern and place of their work to make it more compatible with family life. Doctors are passing up promotions in favor of small-town, family practice. Professional persons are choosing options that allow them to include their families in the activities of their work. Parents are seeking greater control over work schedules, and more flexibility in caring for their children by working closer to home. Work at home seems the optimum solution, especially for parents of young children.

What we are seeing today is not new; it is a shift back toward patterns of work which prevailed before the industrial revolution and the rise of factories. Women then shared fully in the productive cycles of labor while raising children. Work and child care were integrated. The home was a busy hub of activity. Only since the 19th century has full-time, exclusive motherhood become almost a religious obsession.

If the idea of motherhood as the exclusive occupation for a woman seems religious, it is hardly biblical. The noble wife praised in Proverbs 31 works with eager hands, considers a field and buys it, and out of her earnings she plants a vineyard. She opens her arms to the poor and extends her hands to the needy. She is clothed with strength and dignity; she speaks with wisdom and faithful instruction is on her tongue. Above all, such a woman "who fears the Lord is to be praised." She is an intelligent manager at home, but her ministry also extends far beyond her home.

We know other women in the Bible who were active outside the home. Deborah was a political leader; Phoebe and Priscilla and Philip's daughters were religious leaders; Lydia was a businesswoman. You may think such women weird or exceptional. I am convinced they were visionary pacesetters in a way God wants more of us to go.

"Housekeeping" in itself is a dead-end. The advertising folks try to keep women preoccupied with their house and with making themselves attractive to men. Despite rises in living standards and increases in labor-saving devices, women tend to spend more time on home chores.[17] American advertisers love empty-headed women with expensive tastes and a penchant for collecting gadgets for their cluttered homes. Most of these devices are consumptive dead-ends, designed to gobble up our time and waste our spirits!

Our homes are to be instruments of ministry and mercy to those in need, not exhibition halls for our finery. Unless we deliberately keep our housekeeping simple, we can too soon become obsessed with trivial pursuits that empty our heads and our hearts (as well as our wallets). Paul wrote to the Romans: "Do not conform any longer to the pattern of this world, but be transformed by the renewing of your mind" (12:2).

It is suggested that, whereas the central failing for males is pride or the "will to power," women tend "to sin by triviality and diffuseness—by underdevelopment of the self, rather than overdevelopment."[18]

Is the woman's place in the home, as traditionalists are fond of claiming? Certainly home is one important arena for ministry when there are persons there who need her. In that case, home may well be the man's place, too. Our real ministry does begin in our home. That ministry also extends beyond the home. Back when lives were shorter and families larger, mothering may have been a lifetime occupation. Today, however, things are different in important ways.

If the ordinary family now has two children, full-time care for them in their early years spans only about ten years at most. Even as a concentrated effort, this is only half a life-work. And a big part of doing it well is to work oneself out of the job, preparing children for interaction with others and ultimately for independence.

The role of mother ends. Women who devoted themselves most exclusively to it are liable to suffer most when the children "fly the nest." But women who have consistently thought of motherhood as part of a larger plan for their lives have a head start on extending their ministries into other spheres at this stage. The circle of concern and caring widens to include others. Our schools and communities and a multitude of worthy projects benefit from the enlarged scope of a mother's activities.

Biblical feminists enjoy being mothers and wives, but our ultimate identities are larger than that. We are first of all disciples of Jesus Christ. Other roles and activities flow from that relationship.

Jesus commended Mary of Bethany for choosing to sit at his feet. He rebuked Martha for her preoccupation with the hostess role. Jesus wasn't devaluing Martha's service, but was attempting to free her from the worry and distraction of social proprieties. He implied that spiritual and mental growth are more important than perfect hospitality. Jesus was not denying that we must eat, sleep, and care for our physical needs. He put the *emphasis* somewhere else. "Mary has chosen what is better, and it will not be taken away from her" (Luke 10:42).

Jesus broke down walls of prejudice and opened new vistas of hope for women. He treated women with dignity and respect. He taught them profound theological truths. A woman is not honored in God's sight for giving birth, he taught, but for hearing the Word of the Lord and keeping it. He encouraged women to minister, to proclaim the good news far and wide.

Jesus' good news transformed woman after woman, restoring human dignity to many who had been utterly crushed by a cruel, sexist culture and legal system. As women caught the vision, they moved with passion and ecstatic joy to tell everyone of Jesus, their liberator. Captivated by his outpouring of love and forgiveness, they gave up everything just to be with this Savior who had restored them to wholeness. Jesus had liberated them from bondage to disease, death, and hypocritical men. The mighty Lord, the Prince of Peace, the wonderful Counselor had walked among them and raised them up.

Every child of God is gifted. All good gifts come from God and are intended to be used in building up the body of Christ. Our life in the new society of Christ is rooted in grace, not in gender-based restrictions. Again, Paul wrote the Romans: "Having gifts that differ according to the grace given to us, let us use them" (12:6).

The kingdom of God is no place for *false* humility. Gifts are not to be ignored or denied. To belittle them is to quench and grieve the Spirit of the Giver.

Homes and families have too often been a convenient excuse for turning our backs on others. We want to be left alone to look to our own secure, padded dens. In fairness, I must admit that young mothers and fathers are typically too exhausted to reach far beyond themselves in ministering to others. But immediate demands must always be seen within the larger panorama. Like the ripples in a pond, our willingness to share love with the smallest ones radiates out to touch others also.

On the dark side, fathers and mothers who have never learned to minister to the people closest to them at home, will not likely minister well to the many others out there.

There is so much work to be done in our world. We need more women like Dorcas, Deborah, Lydia, Esther, Rahab, Miriam, Rachel, Elizabeth, Mary, and Priscilla. Women bring unique gifts to leadership responsibilities. Just as women's gifts have benefited the home and family, so women's strengths can provide a unique contribution in service to institutions. Fresh from years of intensive support for high-quality relationships, women emerging from parental tasks bring a concern for persons as well as smooth functioning, an appreciation for relational qualities as well as efficiency, and an ability to work for consensual decisions rather than within hierarchical patterns.

Women, where have our lives come from? Where are we going? We possess an unspeakable desire to be all that we were created to be. In Jesus we find the freedom that we yearn for, the "true, original course" for which we seek. We are not particularly blessed for being mothers, or professionals, for being single or married. Blessedness comes in doing the will of God with all the fire and restless force that throbs within our hearts!

11

Empathy

Walk a While in My Shoes

Is this a holy thing to see
In a rich and fruitful land,
Babes reduc'd to misery,
Fed with cold and usurous hand?

Is that trembling cry a song?
Can it be a song of joy?
And so many children poor?
It is a land of poverty!
—*William Blake*[1]

Timothy yelled with full-throated fury. Hunger pains in his knotted stomach turned my adorable, cuddly bundle into a livid, enraged dynamo. As I rushed to throw together a nourishing gruel and fill his bottle, I remembered the millions of nameless starving babies I had often read about. Such a mind-numbing mass of starving humanity usually aroused a faint pity within me, but it really was all so incomprehensible and so far away.

Yet as my own baby agonized in hunger for a mere five minutes, stark, debilitating starvation marched into my mind with new momentum. When other babies wailed out their distant cries the sound signified anonymous babies crying. My baby's cry bespoke an urgent, desperate plea for help!

My heart grew heavy with gratitude as I listened to Timothy gurgling down life-giving milk to fill his aching belly. His wide eyes softened with contentment and he nestled against my chest. I understood as never before that when a mother is unable to provide food and medical care for her little ones, it is the cruelest of tragedies!

Becoming a mother has sensitized me to the suffering of millions of mothers and their little ones. In a significant way, motherhood has humanized me, making me more aware of basic human need. Most women become mothers with little or no choice in the matter. The condition of a majority of pregnant women in our world is that of poverty and malnutrition.

There is an enormous difference between struggling to survive and striving to be fulfilled. It is too easy for those of us who consider ourselves feminists to concentrate on our own fulfillment and to forget that mere survival preoccupies so many of the world's women. What do I have in common with a woman whose child died because no penicillin was available? How am I like the mother whose malnourished baby lies listlessly with distended belly and sticklike limbs on her lap because she has nothing to feed him?

From one perspective we have nothing in common: different cultures, different social class, different religious expression, different aesthetic tastes. Yet from another point of view, we have everything in common: our bodies, our physical needs, our motherhood, our desire to provide for our helpless child, our humanity. The same pride, greed, and selfishness that have so often prevented women from expressing their gifts in all arenas of our society are at root responsible for the dehumanizing conditions of poverty that plague vast regions of our world. There is a pattern in the domination and exploitation, the rape of the Third World, the violation of land and water, the racism, war, and sexism of our world systems.

The gaunt eyes of mother and child peer out of photographs at the unheeding gluttony of the American public. We don't bring much comprehension to the needs of the hungry, because we don't understand the roots of sexism in our churches or the oppressive patterns in our homes. The desire to lord it over others, to enjoy the fruits of domination and control—this is the root cause of poverty, poverty of body and of spirit.

With the Hebrew prophet Hosea we hear an enraged God rebuking Israel: "When I fed them, they were satisfied; when they were satisfied, they became proud; then they forgot me. So I will come upon them like a lion, like a leopard I will lurk by the path. Like a bear robbed of her cubs, I will attack them and rip them open" (Hosea 13:6-8).

God identifies with the enraged mother bear whose cubs have been taken away. God pursues their captors with a vengeance that surpasses the anger of every mother in our world whose little ones have been robbed of food, of health care, of a chance to live, love, and laugh. "I tell you the truth," Jesus said, "whatever you did not do for one of the least of these, you did not do for me." Those who care for the least of these are rewarded with eternal life, Jesus declared. Those who disdain, disregard, or merely tolerate the least of these are damned to eternal punishment.

A mother's battle for her child must become a common human battle. Each of us can do only a small, small part, but when we join hands in the struggle against poverty, war, exploitation, and callousness we shed abroad a glimmer of hope. Survival is, after all, a shared struggle. No man or woman is an island, complete unto itself, as John Donne wrote centuries ago. Each person's joys and sorrows are intertwined with another's, so that when one suffers it touches the life of every person.

The suffering of children, especially, should shatter our complacency. When we look at children, writes Philip Hallie in *Lest Innocent Blood Be Shed,* we feel what Gerard Manley Hopkins was expressing in his poem, "Spring," when he wrote, "What is all this juice and all this joy?"[2]

"Children are the springtime, the creative burgeoning of human life," avows Hallie. They breathe vitality into those around them. When they are tortured or deliberately broken, it is spring being attacked. The "living center of human life" is dirtied and smashed when children are harmed. There is an "unbridgeable difference," Hallie contends, between those who can destroy children (or allow it) and those who can only save them.[3]

For those who believe that human life is precious beyond price, there are, as C. S. Lewis declares, no *ordinary* people.[4] Nobody, not even the alcoholic wasted on skid row or the child beggar on a Calcutta street, nobody is a "mere mortal." We are all valued beyond any material assessment of worth; we have the spark of eternity and the light of God's radiant image within. Yet we treat each other as if we were dumb, dusty cattle.

On this day 35,000 children under five years of age will die from hunger and hunger-related diseases. TODAY! That is 13,000,000 who die within a single year.[5] Such numbers render us incapable of comprehending the depth of tragedy. More profoundly, they devalue human worth in every sphere. While human beings die like so many flies, we salve our senses by rationalizing that they are not the lofty, enlightened creatures that we consider ourselves to be.

No, we think, the destiny of the starving seems tied somehow to the animal world where only the fittest survive. Enthroned in privilege, we blame the victims for their own deaths. Perhaps we don't really mind that children are starving as long as they don't interfere with *our* success or comfort. Instead of loving our neighbors as ourselves we clamor for our government to spend more to protect *our* privilege. Rather than entering into full compassionate solidarity with those who suffer, we prefer to support a national security policy that builds dividing walls between the favored few and the unfortunate many.

In 1978, the developed nations spent 20 times more for their military programs than they did for economic aid to poorer countries. In two days the world spends on arms as much as it allots to the United Nations for an entire year. Although more than 1,500,000,000 people lack access to professional health services, and over 1,400,000,000 have no safe drinking water, and over 500,000,000 suffer from malnutrition, world governments spend twice as much on arms as they do on health care.[6]

Oh, please, you may implore, don't throw all those depressing facts at us again. We've heard them so often. There is no solution. There is no way to turn the superpowers around, no method to turn armaments into food when people are obsessed with "national security."

I too am stymied and paralyzed in the face of global poverty and hunger. Nothing I can do would make a substantial difference out there. I will admit, however, that my heart has changed, softened, and grown more tender. As a woman and a mother I feel more able, along with other women, to identify with the travail of those who crave bread and dignity. If there is one group in our country who can empathize with the poor and oppressed, it is women. It is we who can most compassionately share the suffering of our sisters around the world, we can identify with their longing to provide a decent life for their children.

The women of our world are often the downtrodden of the downtrodden. If you are poor or hungry, the chances are that you will be poorer or hungrier if you are also female. A woman is sole provider in one quarter to one third of the households in the world, and most of these are among the poorest people, in the poorest societies.[7] Most of the world's farmers are women, yet women as a group suffer most from inadequate food supplies. Technological improvements in agriculture have most often been applied to the cash crops raised by men for export, not to the food crops raised by women for their families.[8]

Prime agricultural land is bought up by multinational corporations which make enormous profits on luxury foods grown in poor countries and exported to rich countries. The many women and men working to eke out enough food for their hungry children are pushed to the fringes and bullied by these corporations. The consensus of experts is that the only way to wipe out hunger is to increase the agricultural production of hundreds of millions of small farmers, most of whom are women.

Hunger will not disappear until we are able to deal with the fact that the present economy, taken as a global system, thrives on the poor. The poor are the price paid for the wealth, power, comfort, and control enjoyed by the non-poor.[9]

What can we do? Because our hearts have been softened by the anguish of the poor, we can refuse to wear the blinders that kept us from seeing the malignant self-interest that has turned our society to narcissistic consumption. We can turn a deaf ear to the militarist leaders who value armaments above human dignity. We can, in our consciences, allow the eyes of hungry children to watch us as we shop for groceries and sit down to full meals.

We can root for the small farmer whose little plot of land is the key to wiping out hunger. We can fast from time to time and so become sensitive to the true significance of food. We can repent of our callousness, and of our temptation to despair. We can open our ears and hearts to the poor. "If a man shuts his ears to the cry of the poor, he too will cry out and not be answered" (Proverbs 21:13).

We can evangelize each other in the ways of God's love, relaxing our clutching instincts and revitalizing our resolve to give. "If anyone has material possessions and sees his brother in need but has no pity on him, how can the love of God be in him?" (1 John 3:17).

I have often heard a particular verse used in evangelistic settings: "Here I am! I stand at the door and knock. If anyone hears my voice and opens the door, I will go in and *eat with him*, and he with me" (Revelation 3:20, italics added). The emphasis given from the pulpit was usually on the door as the heart; opening it meant conversion. Recently I have sensed how significant the eating is. Jesus highlighted the centrality and goodness of table fellowship. Eating together was Jesus' way of expressing human aspirations and satisfying basic human needs.[10]

Jesus performed his first miracle while eating and drinking with others at a wedding celebration. In his final moments Jesus shared a last supper with his friends, offering up his own body as the bread and wine of the first communion meal. It was as Jesus broke bread that his friends recognized him in Emmaus. Jesus compared the kingdom of heaven to a man who gave a great banquet, implying that people eating together is a sign of the kingdom.

Eating is fundamentally an experience of bringing people together. Hunger and partaking of food is a commanding experience which orders all else and makes each of us what we are. Sharing food is unlike sharing anything else, because food is so closely bound up with life itself.[11] If we do not have food, we do not have life. It's that simple!

It follows then that one of the minimum conditions making human life worthwhile is a family eating together. If you have rice and family around you, you are not poor. If you do not have them, you are poor. The desire of the poor is to eat with their families. "Eating together is the opposite of poverty."[12] Making it possible for families to eat together is what the battle against poverty is all about.

Hunger is preventable. Human expertise could produce enough food for people all over the world to eat with their families. Gandhi asserted that there is enough in our world for everyone's need, but not for everyone's greed. Our four-year-old Joseph arrived at his own explanation: "Rich people are like robbers."

If eating together with loved ones is a minimum condition, it is also a maximum, for life offers nothing more beautiful. [13] That is why Jesus longs to come through the door and *eat* with us. He desires to satisfy our needs, to share with us the bread of life, the source of temporal and eternal life.

Jesus knew that when we are surrounded by luxury and abundance we lose our sense of true dependence on our Creator. Consequently he said, "Do not worry, saying, 'What shall we eat?' or 'What shall we drink?' or 'What shall we wear?' For the pagans run after all these things, and your heavenly Father knows that you need them. But seek first his kingdom and his righteousness, and all these things will be given to you as well" (Matthew 6:31-33).

Surrounded by affluence, we regularly gobble our food without thought for the good Giver. But when we live on the poverty line, every morsel of bread for the hungry mouths of our children is cause for thanksgiving.

The birth of our boys forced me toward a new dependence on the goodness of the Giver. Their presence in my life made me vulnerable to a whole new dimension of pain and suffering. I cannot guarantee that they will never know hunger, that they will never be abducted or injured in accident or war. I cannot promise that they will never be parentless or terminally ill. I cannot even tell them that bombs and shells only fall in distant strife-torn lands, when a nuclear bomb could annihilate us all at any moment.

Joseph used to ask regularly at bedtime, "Mama, will the monsters get me?" I would reassure him, kid him, and give him a hug. We often laughed together with the sure word that there are no monsters and so of course they can't get him.

Then one night he asked about kidnappers who take children from their parents. I longed for the comfy "monster" catch-all that we had until then laid to rest each night. Now came a critical test of faith for me.

I had read the hideous statistics: a million youngsters disappear in the United States every year, with as many as 50,000 of them still missing a year later. Hundreds of unidentified bodies of children are found each year. And most gruesome are the 20 percent of abducted children who are sold in adoption rings or abused in the child pornography "industry."

When bombarded by extensive news coverage of missing children and agonizing parents, I wished for the first time that I had never given birth. In answering Joseph about kidnappers, I only offered reassurance. I wouldn't bespeak my misgivings. Yet as my mind probed into the terror of a small child subjected to brutal molestation, I stumbled in faith. Where is God when the innocent suffer?

The world seems so horrific at times; my power to protect my "cubs" appears meager indeed. When we chose to give birth I hadn't fathomed how it would tear my heart every time I hear of another child's broken body. I hadn't reckoned on the aching void of faith that would overwhelm me when fear for my own trusting innocents grows unchecked within. I hadn't comprehended how devastated children would be when forced to watch their own parents tortured and killed.

"It's really scary if mama and daddy die before the little boy does," Joseph said recently. "I can't live all by myself. Who will take care of me?" he wondered. Generally happy and confident, Joseph is also sensitive and aware.

The children of Lebanon have seen their mothers and fathers slaughtered. Many have lost all sense of security. About 6,000 orphans are known to be in public or private institutions in Lebanon and that is only the tip of the iceberg.

In Central America countless children live in constant terror as battles rage, their fathers and brothers are carted off to be tortured and killed, and their families forced to flee.

Crimes against children as reported in North American papers seem to be more and more vicious. Perhaps it was because I had been out of the United States for six odd years in a relatively crime-free society that I was so taken aback by the alarming stories of child abuse. It is now estimated that one out of four children in the United States has been sexually molested, and that half of those doing the abusing are not strangers but persons to whom parents have entrusted their children, or the parents themselves.

According to the American Humane Association there were almost 48,000 reported cases of incest in 1982. Henry Giaretto, a psychologist and founder of a child sexual abuse treatment program, insists that this figure is far too low. He estimates that more than 250,000 children in this country are sexually molested in their homes each year. (Approximately 85 percent of incest victims are female, according to the American Humane Association. Father-daughter incest accounts for 75 percent of the reported cases.)[14]

Violent child abuse is probably the number one killer of children in America, ranking above infectious diseases, leukemia, or car accidents. Up to 4,000 children are killed each year *by their parents* in our society. About 60,000 children suffer dangerously from beatings, cruelty, or neglect at home.[15]

Where do we turn for comfort? The Lord says, "As a mother comforts her child, so will I comfort you" (Isaiah 66:13). When I see my child in every little one whose frightened eyes search for food, for safety, for love, I silently weep. Why do the innocent suffer? Certainly that is the thorniest question that has ever confronted theologians. The suffering of children is the most bitter fruit of wickedness. The principalities and powers of darkness strive with malicious fervor to dim and extinguish the light of life that burns in the eyes of our children.

Ivan, in *Brothers Karamazov*, probes the question with near intolerable clarity:

> I recognize in all humility that I cannot understand why the world is arranged as it is. Men are themselves to blame, I suppose: they were given paradise, they wanted freedom....
>
> But then there are the children, and what am I to do about them? That's the question I can't answer.... Listen! If all must suffer to pay for eternal harmony, what have children to do with it? Tell me please. It's beyond all comprehension why they should suffer and why they should pay for the harmony.... It's not worth the tears of that one tortured child who beat itself on the breast with its little fist ... with its tears to 'dear, kind God'!.... If the sufferings of children go to swell the sum of sufferings which are necessary to pay for truth, then I protest that the truth is not worth such a price.[16]

There is one, we believe, whose innocent blood was shed to atone for all and everything. Ultimately, because of his sacrifice, justice will roll down like waters in the desert and we will cry out, "Great and marvelous are your deeds, Lord God Almighty. Just and true are your ways, King of the ages.... Worthy is the Lamb, who was slain, to receive power and wealth and wisdom and strength and honor and glory and praise!" (Revelation 15:3 and 5:12).

Now, though, more often than not, we are weak-kneed and filled with doubt. Even though Jesus said, "Let the little children come to me, and do not hinder them, for the kingdom of God belongs to such as these," the children always seem to suffer the most.

On the surface we are a nation that adores children, but our government spends billions of dollars "defending their freedom" instead of providing adequate food and housing and health care. We spend endless sums of money for our security and our survival, but our very future in the human potential of our children is woefully neglected. The same government that would substitute ketchup for vegetables in school lunches to save money will find ways to spend $436 for a $7 hammer, millions of dollars for an invasion of Grenada, and billions of dollars for extending the arms race into space. Who needs enemies?

One fourth of all children in the United States are poor, and children make up 40 percent of the poverty population. A 1984 report of the Children's Defense Fund states that children in this country "are significantly poorer, more likely to suffer death and sickness, hunger and cold, abuse and neglect and inadequate child care" than four years earlier. "They are less likely to be born with adequate prenatal care, to be immunized, have access to preventive health and dental care, and to receive supplemental education services" than in 1980.[17]

Nothing but the best for the children, but we insult them with the emptiest entertainment imaginable. We desensitize them with television violence and greed. (More power to the rare exceptions, those few wholesome shows for kids!) We treat our children as objects whose affections are manipulated for the pleasure of adults. We are often so absent from their lives that we try to fill the gap with toys and trinkets. Otherwise normal adults not too long ago fought each other for places in overnight lines waiting to snatch up the current status symbol of parental affection for their children, "Cabbage Patch" dolls.

In many ways we have become an anti-child culture. The public is outraged over welfare expenditures, but no one defends the children who depend on this public aid. We say we cherish our children yet we pay teachers and child care workers poorly, while far less crucial jobs are rewarded much more highly. In my estimation, teachers and child care workers should be paid higher wages than *any other profession*. This would attract more qualified people to give children the kind of care they deserve. Then our appreciation for children would have more substance!

As the work force expands to include more and more mothers, the burdens of this social change have too often fallen on children. The well salaried job market often draws the most qualified persons out of child care settings and their place in the home and day-care centers is taken by less qualified persons. During the years when a child must learn trust and self-worth, many day-care centers are so impersonal that their main lesson for the child is survival tactics!

Many babies are "warehoused" for ten hours each day with an indifferent, overworked care-giver, whose qualifications may be very low. Most severely endangered are the children in poverty whose mothers must work at paid employment and who are cared for by strangers in what amounts to storage houses.[18]

Full-time day-care is definitely not preferable for children under three years of age, whose parents are capable of caring for them. However, a pleasant, well-staffed, and well-funded day-care center should be available at reasonable cost for those who are in desperate need. The single parent, the financially strapped parent, the immature and hostile parent ought to be given the option of putting their children into an attractive, affordable day-care setting.

One innovative day-care idea which I like is to combine care for the young with care for the elderly. Many older folks in institutions would welcome the opportunity to help youngsters in need of love. The stories they could swap would be therapeutic for all involved. The little ones would learn to love and appreciate the special charm and gentleness of the elderly.

Those of us who *can* spend a lot of time at home with our children welcome part-time day-care or shared child care options to provide us with personal space and relief. A support group of parents and people who love children makes a tremendous difference in one's attitude toward parenting. Children's needs are less likely to be neglected when their parents' needs for support, friendship, and creative work are being met. In our culture, more than in many other cultures, parents are expected to go it alone. This is impossible. New parents are under tremendous stress; they need their own sources of nurture to keep going.

It terrifies me to think that we *can* destroy our children. If we have no place where it is safe to admit to our negative, hostile feelings, we are all the more likely to take these tensions out on our children. Our anxieties can be reduced if we are able to exchange information and worries with other parents and reassure each other that our responses are within the range of normalcy.

The nuclear family in isolation is really an impractical arrangement. Instead of leading to independence and freedom, its intense self-reliance can actually hinder individual liberty. A loose cooperative of three or four families would be better for raising children together. Within extended family groupings where child care can be shared, it becomes more feasible for mothers and fathers to continue their study or work part-time in gainful employment. In addition to benefiting the parents, such an arrangement enables our children to be with many trusted adults, and to know a larger circle of caring persons.

Our sons have known more than their share of sorrowful partings from friends and loved ones. As farewells were shared, Joseph, with tears streaming down his face repeatedly cried, "Oh, I don't like to leave my friends. I wish everyone could live in the same big house. Then we'd *never* have to leave and say good-bye!"

Joseph's longing reminded me of Jesus' words, "In my Father's house are many rooms; if it were not so, I would have told you. I am going there to prepare a place for you" (John 14:2). In longing to share life within the context of a harmonious household of loving, fascinating people, where children enjoy good friendships and work loads are eased, we are led toward a utopian dream. Most of us don't imagine we could get along well with others in such close quarters. It seems we prefer the strain of going it alone to the stress of continual negotiation within a bustling household. And yet this desire for harmonious community continues to throb among us. A community in which persons care about us and our children and in which we too care for others is essential for the well-being of our families!

Gerald and I are now members of a worshiping community of people who live within several blocks of each other in Evanston, Illinois. Our commitment to each other involves an encompassing love for each other's children. We actively structure child care sharing arrangements to lighten our loads and delight our children. Part of our commitment to God is the forthright intention to nurture each other's children, to join together in providing a more wholesome, enriching environment for our daughters and sons than any of us could provide on our own.

Dr. Brazelton noted that he longs for the revival of two customs in our culture which are strengths within other cultures. The first custom he advocates is for mothers to allow themselves more continual physical closeness with their infants. And his second desire is to see a resurgence of the extended family for cushioning and supporting young parents. A strong culture, he says, emphasizes the value of the extended family as a backup and a conveyer of customs and values to inexperienced parents.[19]

In a broader perspective, the rights of children are receiving new attention. We are witnessing the slow, quiet beginnings of a "children's liberation" movement. A pendulum may be swinging slowly in the direction of a family way of life again. Only recently in our civilization have we become aware of children as "special persons" who require extraordinary attention and nurture. Our understanding of "child development" and the quality of a child's life has improved dramatically in recent decades. Many children still suffer today, but there is a societal concern to alleviate that suffering that did not exist years ago.[20]

No other principle should be more important in unifying our social programs than our children's right to be with those who love and cherish them. Can the child development experts, the women's liberation forces, and the family pull in the same direction? When we transform our ideal of work and our ideal of family, affirming the importance of both, we can create social solutions in which men, women, and children can be liberated together. The bottom line is that nobody, especially not the children, should have to pay the price for another's fulfillment.

I have confessed that I was anti-child before I became a mother, even though not in an outspoken or deliberate way. No. Mine was a closely guarded, subtle pity for the tired woman whose pregnant belly announced her fate. Mine was the secret disdain for kids who could not sit still or mind their own business. Only when I began to experience the pitying and deprecating stares of others at my own enlarged abdomen did I lift my arm to salute women who dare to carry a child with dignity. Only when my own heart broke to think that pain might strike down my child did it begin to pound with admiration for parents who rise with resilient courage above the forces that grind them down in poverty.

When I held my helpless infant, it was almost as if nothing else *mattered*. As I allowed the well-being of my child to move me to nurture life, I was strengthened in my commitment to minister to every child whom I encounter. Every child has a right to be wanted, fed, and surrounded by family in a society that values that child's well-being above all.

The political conservatives who are responsible for tremendous reductions in programs that benefit children seem to be most concerned with children from the moment of conception to the time of birth. Their spokespersons show compassion for the 15 million fetuses aborted in the last 11 years, but where is their concern for the 13 million children living in poverty whose hopes for the future are snuffed out and whose lives are filled with real pain? Political liberals who defend a woman's right to abort appear to be more concerned to maintain that "right" than with fostering a sense of responsibility for healthy family life.[21]

Being "pro-family" in our day must mean that we work as families to change the very structure of society, freeing parents to give quality *and* quantity time to children. It means we must motivate our most qualified adults to provide leadership in day-care centers and schools. We must work, pray, and share so that all families can partake of food around the table together. Instead of pouring our money into armaments, we must show our concern for national security by surrounding our *greatest national resource*, our children, with the loving arms of their nearest and dearest.

"Mama, did you want me before I was born?" Joseph asked one day.

"Yes," I answered. The misgivings about possible suffering that flicker across my heart didn't dim the truth that he was wanted and is dearly loved. Little did he or I know that his birth would so gentle my heart that I would grow to ache for and cherish many other children too.

Our children were not given us so that we could dote on them and brag about their accomplishments. The task is bigger than the preservation of our own family alone. Because of our children and with our children, we are enabled more sensitively to reach out to other children and other families who long for fellowship. "Let the little children come to me."

12

Conversion

Become as Little Children

in the beginning
there is a child
and that child continues
        in us all

we are that child
and when we accept this discovery
the child develops
        and teaches us
up through time

the child is father and mother of us all
this is both fact
and the beginning of wisdom.
        —*Joe Pearson*[1]

Joseph used to say to me, "When you get little like I am . . . ." My response was a chuckle and a lighthearted explanation that he had it all backwards. On further reflection, however, he may have been closer to the truth than I was. I have grown wiser to the verity that unless we adults "get little" we can never hope to become full-fledged members of the kingdom. Jesus put it most disturbingly: "Unless you change and become like little children, you will *never* enter the kingdom of heaven" (Matthew 18:3, italics added). I wonder if any of us have become "little" enough to know what he meant.

Children have become for me a primary impulse toward conversion. While stooping to relate to their needs and pleasures, I have entered new realms of understanding and freedom. Little children in an endearing way bring out the child in us if we let them. "They can and do, if you give them half a chance, make a dent in the toughest armour of life. If you're very lucky they can dissolve away all those protective barricades so carefully erected over years of living."[2]

More than making a dent in my armor, my sons have quite disarmed me. More than being a distraction on my road to bigger and better things, they have become a central part of God's transforming grace in my life.

Adults have a hankering to appear as if they have it all together. We strain to achieve a logical, hypocritical perfection that orders our world and controls our responses. Our arrogance, our self-righteousness, our proper and principled behavior all get in the way of loving children and becoming like children.

I have noted with great delight on different occasions how pompous, tight-lipped dignitaries melt in the presence of children. I think of one church leader who carried himself stiffly, requesting that everyone address him only with formal titles of respect. Chummy familiarity was taboo with that man. But to see him with his grandchildren was to see a man reborn. He played, laughed, and relaxed. His grandchildren adored him, while the church folk found him difficult, evasive, and even deceitful.

Another "man of the collar" was silent, distant, and not easy to communicate with. Yet when children approached him, he let down his guard, did crazy antics, and laughed aloud. He was at his most amusing and lovable when he was freely frolicking with small children. In adult company a cloak of silence covered his spontaneity and muffled his responsiveness.

Little children shatter our facades. With affection and charm they snuggle against our aching, lonely hearts and accept us for what we are, not for what we strain to be. They unmask our adult reserve and make it possible for us to say more nearly what we feel deep inside. Like persistent woodpeckers they bore through our crusty callousness and release the pent-up part of us that longs for birth, for play, for wings.

Oscar Wilde penned a delightful story called *The Selfish Giant*. It tells of a giant who had a lovely garden where children loved to play. But the giant said, "My own garden is my own garden, anyone can understand that, and I will allow nobody to play in it but myself." Whereupon, he walled the children out. Snow and frost took up permanent residence in the garden.

But one day the children crept back into the garden. In each tree where a child sat, blossoms burst forth and birds twittered. Only one tree continued to be covered with frost and snow. The little boy beneath it was in tears, because he couldn't climb up into its branches.

The giant's heart melted as he looked out at his garden. "How selfish I have been!" he said. "Now I know why the spring would not come here. I will put that poor little boy on the top of the tree, and then I will knock down the wall, and my garden shall be the children's playground for ever and ever." The last tree burst into blossom and the little boy, sitting on its branches, stretched out his arms, and flung them around the giant's neck and kissed him.

The giant loved that boy best, because he had kissed him, but he never saw him again, until the day the giant died. Then the boy came, now with nail prints on his palms, and said to the giant, "You let me play once in your garden. Today you shall come with me to my garden, which is paradise."[3]

It was Jesus who said, "Whoever welcomes a little child like this in my name welcomes me" (Matthew 18:5). God seems to be fond of "limiting" himself to little people. "Whatever you did for one of the least of these . . . you did for me" (Matthew 25:40).

He chose to be born of Mary in a stable. He sends blessings to the have-nots, and woes to the comfortable. The poor people, the despised publicans, and the harlots were more apt to welcome him than were the priests and merchants. When Jesus wanted to illustrate what it takes to enter the kingdom, he did not choose outstanding religious leaders as examples. Nor did he lift up patriarchal fathers or charitable businessmen to be emulated. He chose a child to exemplify those who may enter his kingdom, and those who are the greatest in his kingdom.

Gerald and I like fantasy literature; we are eagerly introducing it to our sons. Joseph has a special place in his heart for Bilbo Baggins of *The Hobbit*. The *Chronicles of Narnia*, in which children play a critical role in events and experience Aslan's special favor, are among Joseph's most dearly loved stories.

The heroes in fantasy are rarely the powerful, the highly respected, or the noble classes. With regularity, the great people in fantasy are the weak or the small or the disregarded members of their society. Yet these little people are enormously effective against evil. Not princes, nor sorcerers or other sophisticates, but hobbits are the ones able to fight dark lords and overcome.[4]

What is so special about little people? Are children really so far ahead of us in grasping the true essence of the kingdom, as Jesus seems to indicate? I continue to wonder what Jesus meant by telling us to become like children. What particular childlike aspects are we to emulate? Certainly not all of them!

Henri Nouwen in an article called "The Selfless Way of Christ" sheds some light, I think, on what it means to be childlike:

> The great paradox which Scripture reveals to us is that real and total freedom can only be found through downward mobility. The Word of God came down to us and lived among us as a slave.... Somewhere deep in our hearts we already know that success, fame, influence, power, and money do not give us the inner joy and peace for which we crave. Somewhere we can even sense a certain envy of those who have shed all their ambitions and live their lives in simple obedience. Yes, somewhere we can even get a taste of that mysterious joy in the smile of those who have nothing to lose.[5]

Children aren't preoccupied by success, fame, and money. We envy their carefree skips and their trusting embrace. In watching our children we learn what it is to be a child of God. We are children in God's family, and God is our *ultimate parent*.

In our need, our dependency, our vulnerability, we seek for our fathering and mothering God to strengthen us, love us, affirm us. It is not easy to be a child before God. We would much rather have our own affairs well in hand. Ultimately, though, we come to God with empty hands, desperately needing what only God can provide! We come mysteriously joyful, because we have nothing to lose and everything to receive from the Source of all that is good!

Joseph declared the other day that he didn't ever want to grow up, because grown-ups don't play much. We tried to assure him that adults do like to play. After all, aren't his mom and dad prime examples?

Well, apparently not, at least not on that particular day. A few days later his tune had changed. With fervor he announced: "I like being a kid so much! When I grow up to be a man, I still want to have some child-spirit in me!" Chalk one up for the beginning of wisdom.

There's a vast difference between knowledge and wisdom. Growing small, becoming a child, and befriending children have everything to do with acquiring wisdom and true understanding. When the children were shouting in the temple, "Hosanna to the Son of David," the chief priests and teachers of the Law were indignant.

"Do you hear what these children are saying?" they asked Jesus.

"Yes," replied Jesus, "have you never read, 'From the lips of children and infants you have ordained praise'?" (Matthew 21:16).

Jesus was quoting from Psalm 8, where the context is David's poetic praise for God's resplendent handiwork. The knowledgeable chief priests and teachers of the Law were no match for the children's offering of pure praise. Blinded by their education the chief priest and teachers of the Law never approached the wisdom of the very children they disdained.

"O Lord, our Lord, how majestic is your name in all the earth! You have set your glory above the heavens. From the lips of children and infants you have ordained praise..." (Psalm 8:1-2).

My children have restored for me a sense of wonder. I am rediscovering the world through their fresh sensuous perceptions. Their exuberant celebration of sounds, colors, tastes, and beautiful shapes strips the shackles off the boring uniformity of grown-up realities. Staying close to children means staying close to new life, to our own youthful tendencies. Children are our springtime. The invigorating, pulsating life that pushes through crusty sod and tight bud casings inspires even the most sluggish of spirits. When I read what e e cummings wrote of springtime, I sometimes think of children:

> (i who have died am alive again today,
> and this is the sun's birthday; this is the birth
> day of life and of love and wings: and of the gay
> great happening illimitably earth)[6]

There are glorious moments when I look with awe at my child and tingle with pleasure simply because he exists. At such times I'm convinced that the fatigue, anger, and sacrifice have been worth it. Progress of a more formal academic and professional sort has been displaced by the learning which comes only from seeing the world through the eyes of a little person.

Sharing my child's delight in small things and moving things breathes new life into my response to my surroundings. He catches me up into his magical world of discovery, where shadow play brings squeals of laughter, and a flash of lightning is reason to cheer. Excitedly he *insists* that I come out to see a bird singing on the roof peak. In my mind I know it's "only" a house sparrow, but in my heart I know I am celebrating another miracle of God's goodness.

The white petals from the cherry tree blossoms swirl in gusts around us. Joseph wonders why the leaves are falling, if this is spring. I explain, whereupon he immediately wants to go cherry-picking. I rejoice in the infinite complexity and interrelatedness of times and seasons.

The joy of watching new little persons come alive to God's good earth makes being a mother one of the most exquisite pleasures I've known.

"Why does God love us?" Joseph asked.

"Because he made us," I began, with a brief description of the creation.

"Why did he make us out of dirt? I don't want to be out of dirt!" he roundly objected.

"What do you want to be made of?"

"Cherries!"

At such moments I laugh with elation for being human, in spite of dust-to-dust and all the rest. Children put the Ah! back into the mixture of "mess and marvel which makes the mystery of our mortal life."[7] The joys of having children cannot really be explained. A pure, fleeting moment of delight that I share with my son makes me want to hug the world and yell from the rooftops, "All's right with the world!"

There are days when I think I can hardly wait to devour books in peace again, days when I'm so eager to finish the seminary studies I began. There are moments when I desperately want to pour myself wholeheartedly, undistract-edly into work—chaplaincy, teaching, marching for peace—whatever. And then I watch the boys holding hands because the little one is afraid or the little one leaning his head against the older one after hitting him with a drumstick and saying, "Sorry. Please be my best brother"; the little one lay-ing his head on my lap and saying, "I thought we be friends," and his older brother praying, "Help me to be kind and faithful because those are the goodest things to be," and I know my life is rich beyond measure.

These little moments can't be replaced and don't happen at convenient times. Unless we learn to slow down and cherish time with our children, we'll miss the meaning of life. We will have had the experience, as T. S. Eliot warned, but missed the meaning!

Most of us can eat beans and bread for a season, or live in a small apartment and drive a small car to limit our income needs and have more time with our children. We usually need less money than we imagine. We don't need to be bound to the materialistic values of our society. There are things that money can't buy: our children and the simple pleasure of growing little with them and entering into *Life*.

A well-known elderly research psychologist said recently, "If there's any part of my life I'd give anything to do over, it would be to experience, on a day-to-day basis, the pleasure of my children. I guess I thought they would wait to grow up until I'd gotten everything done."[8]

While at one moment I can hardly wait for my sons to grow up and learn independence, the next I'm clinging to each precious moment of the present. All I've got for absolute sure is *one moment*—right now. The future may never come. If I rush pell-mell ahead, I will forever rush through emptiness, because tomorrow, in a very real sense, never comes. We are given today and today alone.

In Thornton Wilder's *Our Town*, Emily Gibbs has just died after giving birth to her second child. She returns to earth to live her twelfth birthday over again. Her mother, bustling about the kitchen, doesn't notice her.

Emily cries out, "Oh Mama, just look at me one minute as though you really saw me.... Just for a moment now we're all together. Mama, just for a moment we're happy. *Let's look at one another."*

Then Emily begins to sob, "I can't go on: It goes so fast. We don't have time to look at one another.... Take me back—up the hill—to my grave. But first: Wait! One more look. Good-by, Good-by world! Good-by, Grover's Corners ... Mama and Papa. Good-by to clocks ticking ... and Mama's sunflowers. And food and coffee. And new-ironed dresses and hot baths ... and sleeping and waking up. Oh, earth, you're too wonderful for anybody to realize you. Do any human beings ever realize life while they live it? Every, every minute?"[9]

Realizing life "every, every minute" reminds me of Paul's instruction: "Be joyful always; pray continually; give thanks in all circumstances, for this is God's will for you in Christ Jesus" (1 Thessalonians 5:16-18).

With my hands in the dishwater I can thank God for dishes, for water, and for the little fellow splashing in the suds beside me. Being free to live fully and know fulfillment doesn't mean that I have arrived at a particular place emotionally, spiritually, or professionally. It means living, becoming, sharing as fully as possible in the time that I have now. Even with children "underfoot" I can meditate, read, sing, create. And sometimes because of the children "in the way" I find a new way that includes the zest and fun that they bring to me in their muddied hands and sparkling eyes.

Almost more than anything else I enjoy sharing with my boys the "magic gateway" of a good book. I am not housebound as long as we can travel together into a world of wonder, beauty, and adventure by reading together. Children's literature connects what is small, delightful, and everyday with what is big, eternal, and true.[10]

Emily Dickinson wrote:

> He ate and drank the precious words,
> His spirit grew robust;
> He knew not more that he was poor,
> Or that his frame was dust.
> He danced along the dingy ways
> And this bequest of wings
> Was but a book. What liberty
> A loosened spirit brings![11]

By reading to our children, we parents are free to travel back to where we once lived as children, reveling in the magic of well-chosen words. Something in the sharing of a good book profoundly connects us with our children. There is nothing so thrilling in our family as the companionship we enjoy around a good story. The more words, stories, and poems a family has in common, the closer they are bound together. Parents who read to their children significantly influence their children to love beauty, truth, and goodness.

As we were reading *Little House on the Prairie*, we all basked in the warmth of a family knit together and overcoming countless obstacles. Joseph asked one eve, "Did this story really happen?"

"Yes," I explained. "Laura was a real woman who wrote

this story about when she was a little girl."

"Laura wrote this book for *me?*" His eyes opened wide with amazement.

"Yes, and for many other children."

"Thank you, Laura. Thank you," Joseph said almost reverently. "I hope Jesus heard me and puts it in Laura's mind that I said thank you."

Reading together sparks good discussions. Children's questions about God and the meaning of life stretch my theological categories and keep me honest. Many a parent has had to think through his or her own religious beliefs anew to answer the questions of a child. I've scrambled many times to come up with a simple but adequate answer which also keeps integrity with my own faith. I still have many questions of my own. Many mysteries remain, for all of us.

We need not give our child the impression that we know all the answers with full clarity. Cultivating a sense of God's mystery, relaxing, and experiencing God are more important than always needing to explain God. It's okay not to under-stand everything. In fact it is more fun to enjoy the wonder of the indescribable than to strain for definitions that package and reduce the truth to mere words.

One day I explained to Joseph that Jesus always was and always will be. Several days later he turned around and said out of the blue, "But Jesus was *made*. In his mother he was *made*."

Well, yes *and* no. What fun! Time for a little theologizing. I love the way children twist and turn our answers, examin-ing them, questioning them, and calling our bluff. In the end more light is shed than if they'd just accepted what we said and closed their window of inquiry.

Gerald was privileged to hear a conversation about God's "three parts" between Joseph and a friend of the same age in the backseat of a small car.

> Friend: "There's the Son and the Father and the Holy Ghost."
> Joseph: "The Holy Ghost? Hey, I never heard of that!"
> Friend: "Yeah, the Holy Ghost."
> Joseph: "No. You can say Holy Ghost or Holy Spirit."
> Friend: "Holy Spirit? Holy?"
> Joseph: "Holy Spirit. Holy Ghost. Holy Monster."
> Friend: "Hah! Holy Monster. Holy Witch. Holy Dragon."
> Joseph: "Holy everything."
> Friend: "Holy car. Holy train track. Holy gitchigoo."
> Joseph: "Hey, don't say those things for God."
> Friend: (hushed tone) "Okay."

I learn from a child's perspective. It is as though he yanks the muffs from my ears and makes me listen again to what I'm really saying. A lot of our religious talk is gibberish. We don't even know what we're saying when we mouth those spiritual-sounding platitudes. Children bring us up short, examine our loose verbiage, and help to bring freshness and integrity back into our worship and prayer.

Children's prayers go to the heart of the matter:

> Jesus, I love you as much as you love me. I try to love you with my whole heart but I have to love someone else too, and you do too.

> Jesus, I'm sad that you're not in this world. You're so far away to help us.... It's so hard being sick. And it's not much fun being sick. Good-night.

> Jesus, make it be night until *you're* ready for morning. I think you like us.

Jesus, thank you that you take care of us and fix our bodies
and everything. Don't let the monsters get me tonight.

The other day Joseph likened God to the Wizard of Oz.
One of my internal responses was, "Let's hope not. Certainly God isn't like a puny man who fools his people with
illusory antics." But Joseph's explanation was very different.
"God is like the Wizard of Oz because he can do wonderful
things for people and make things right, and the city where
he lives is made of precious stones like the Emerald City."

I don't know where my children glean all their understanding of God. Some impressions come from their parents,
some from friends and teachers, some from books we read.
But much of their understanding flows out of the associ-
ations they make on their own as they put the flaming sparks
of truth together in a new and vibrant pattern that speaks to
their need and inspires *their* faith.

It is in our families that we begin to learn that love is the
greatest thing in the world. The well-known educator, Maria
Montessori, said that when children come into the world,
the gift of love is renewed to parents.

> In the depth of this love parents renounce their own lives to
> dedicate them to their children.... It gives them joy and
> does not feel sacrificial.... The efforts parents make for
> their children are a part of parenthood itself. The child
> awakens what adults think of as an ideal; the ideal of renun-
> ciation, of unselfishness, virtues almost unreachable outside
> family life.[12]

Montessori also noted "that Man would degenerate
without the child to help him rise. If the adult does not
waken little by little, a hard crust will form around him and

make him insensible."[13] As we watch a child learn to walk, talk, feed herself, read, and sing, we jump with elation. As the child grows, she touches a fundamental optimism in us. Things *can* progress, *can* grow better because of our work, our love, our devotion.

We learn to live better because we want to love our children better, and in turn love our neighbor and our God better. We don't exist for ourselves alone. Life is "a great gift and a great good," Thomas Merton says, "not because of what it gives us, but because of what it enables us to give to others."[14]

André Trocmé was instrumental in saving countless children's lives during the Nazi occupation of France. Of him it was said that "he kept close to Jesus Christ by helping those who were suffering."[15] Trocmé did what he did because he wanted to be *with* Jesus. I firmly believe that when we are ministering to children we are *with* Jesus in a unique way. In truth, whoever welcomes the little child, welcomes Jesus himself.

And now when I had written most of this chapter, our two-year-old Timothy asked me, "Mama, can you grow little?"

"No, Timothy, I can't."

"Mama, I want you to grow little." He persisted over my objections until I finally hunkered down on my haunches. Then he beamed.

"Mama, there's a tiger coming. I hold your hand. I take care of you. Don't be afraid, Mama."

The truth is, I *am* afraid. I'm afraid of the future. Since becoming "little" I have become more fearful that there will be no future for my children, and for children everywhere. Doomsday scenarios bring the shadow of the end very close.

I cannot promise my children the future, but they have taken my hands and are leading me into it.

The children don't allow me to give in to despair. Their plucky, joyful spirits stir up hope and defiant determination within me. There *will* be a future, because Jesus has the last word, and Jesus is on the side of the children.

13

Hope

Labor Pangs of the New Creation

Behold, we know not anything;
  I can but trust that good shall fall
  At last—far off—at last, to all,
And every winter change to spring.

So runs my dream; but what am I?
  An infant crying in the night;
  An infant crying for the light;
And with no language but a cry.

—Tennyson[1]

We should never have soldiers in our world because soldiers kill doves, and doves are very pretty birds," four-year-old Joseph observed. I couldn't decipher how he arrived at his conclusion but I found within its symbolism a nugget of truth.

Soldiers kill doves. Not only soldiers, but politicians, professionals, church people, and parents do too. How can these things be? More of our money goes to pay for war than to all of our church and educational programs. The enemies out there are imagined to be so evil that defense against them receives our support, our money, and our silent acquiescence.

Some religious people have been moved to praise atomic weapons as "a marvelous gift given to our country by a wise God." The next lines usually have to do with fear of communism, dangers of international terrorism, and determination to maintain existing inequities at the expense of the rest of the world. Our compatriots feel vulnerable knowing that others can obliterate everything we've worked for, saved for, built for all these years. Our houses and careers and families need protection! Close those windows of vulnerability at any cost!

Evil is not incarnate in our enemies alone. Evil resides in the hearts of all who imagine our own security is worth the destruction of another's life. Even if it is only by silence that I condone the preparation and use of nuclear weapons in massive retaliation against "enemies," I have become in my heart, an accomplice in massive murder. If I rely on the Bomb to protect my family and me from harm, I make of it an idol. Unless my security rests in God, I have sold myself to the principalities and powers of darkness.

My children have enabled me to put faces on "enemies," knowing that they too have children. Can I sit idly by as my country points weapons of indiscriminate destruction at Soviet children, who are as delightful, as equal in grace and beauty as my own?

Parents in every society have a strong vested interest in the kind of future which assures peace for all. Gerald and I saw our children play with the children of Communist Party members during our sojourn in Yugoslavia. We sat together at tables, sharing food and jokes and insights. The children enjoyed each other, crossing language barriers and differences in culture more easily than their elders. Up close it is clear that no such differences are worth killing each other over.

"If the war comes, some of the guys might be our friends and we might shoot and kill them, so that's why I don't want to go to the war," Joseph declared one day. I agreed with him.

The United States has stockpiled some 30,000 nuclear weapons, equal to more than 615,000 Hiroshima bombs. The deadly force stored in this country alone is capable of destroying everyone on earth twelve times over. Pope John Paul II said in his first encyclical, March 1979, "We all know well that the areas of misery and hunger on our globe could have been made fertile in a short time, if the gigantic investments for armaments at the service of war and destruction had been changed into investments for food at the service of life."[2]

President Eisenhower admitted, "Every gun that is made, every warship launched, every rocket fired signifies, in the final sense, a theft from those who hunger and are not fed, those who are cold and not clothed. The world in arms is not spending money alone. It is spending the sweat of its laborers, the genius of its scientists, the hopes of its children."[3]

What is to become of the hopes of our children, of Soviet children, of children starving in the developing countries? A macho military mentality continues to dash those hopes. Instead of admitting the huge mistake and turning around, the powers of our world continue to escalate the nightmare, taking the food out of the mouths of hungry children, and robbing all children of a future.

We could, if we really intended to, turn things around. People made this mess, and people can work to reverse it. We must see the two ways set before us this day, the way of life and the way of death. We *can* choose life.

But will we? In the Christian tradition we believe that the kingdom of God is upon us; consequently we repent and act. We believe in the possibility of change. We believe that things do not have to be the way they are!

Even so, it is easy to lose confidence in the future, especially the future facing our children. Most of the time I block the threat from my mind, and try to forget that it exists. But then it hits me—in the middle of the night when m defenses are lowest, or in the first moments of a fresh new morning—a vision of the mushroom cloud, the blast, the rubble, the broken bodies.

Humans have refined the tools of war, incorporating ever more cruel weapons in their deadly arsenals. Horrible, worldwide destruction is closer to activation than ever before. Like the opening of Pandora's box, "civilized" scientific endeavor has given us more total, barbaric, and wanton destruction than any primitive, premodern peoples could have imagined. Who can believe in progress after seeing the atrocities of our century on a scale never matched in previous ages?

Childless friends may well ask how anyone dares to bring a child into a world filled with such formidable unknowns. A different crisis appears on every galloping horse: limited and unpredictable energy supplies, food shortages, a debt-ridden economy, recombined genetics, state terrorism. . . . It's not the horror of unknowns which haunt our children's future so much as the multitude of knowing predictions. One probability study gives our children a single chance in 1,000 of reaching maturity, because of the nuclear threat alone.

To bear a child into such an endangered environment is more than an act of wishful hope. It is an act of defiance, a challenge to the stacked odds. Childbirth is a persistent, taunting defiance of all that is wrong with the world, a recalcitrant affront to the old that must pass away. Birth is ever a renewal of the hope that is to come. Birth has become hope against hope, the stuff of the kingdom not founded in this world. What are those groans of travail Paul heard ringing throughout a creation subject to futility? (Romans 8). Are they birth pangs of a new age, hope of a future yet unseen?

We each entered the world in answer to the inner logic of creation. Each birth is not just another event in an endless cycle of disposable beings. Every new human being must be received by us earlier arrivals as a sign of the other, the new world that will come. Newness of life is truly a gift of the other, "for of such is the kingdom of God."

People birthing children today are not naive about the foreboding odds, and neither are they prone to escapism. Jim Wallis, editor of *Sojourners* magazine, claims that:

> It is precisely because the times are so bad that we need to plant, build and create new life. It could be that the most appropriate response to the growing storm clouds of war is to have and raise children with a determination that they will have a future. To give up is to succumb to despair and unbelief.[4]

The powers of darkness only rejoice when we lose hope. Hope is the substance of faith needed for survival. Hope is the belief that the present situation is not necessary, that things can change. Hope ultimately knows that God rules; the last word is not ours.[5]

What is incredible is that godly men and women persevere. In their individual worlds they continue to hold the forces of evil at bay. The cosmic war between good and evil rages on and on. Ordinary people like you and me wrestle on our own turf to bring more harmony to the cosmic symphony right where we are. Each of us who refuses to give in to apathy and despair can begin to live out new possibilities, sparking around us a movement of hope.

As a mother of two children, I want my boys to know that if humanity destroys their tomorrow, it will be over the strongest objection I could muster. In my home, my work, my neighborhood, and my church I shall do what I can to let a better way emerge. I will strive to embody the way of love, prayer, and gentleness that makes peace visible and viable within my life circle.

The other day Joseph showed me a picture of a full-blown tulip he'd made at nursery school. He asked for paper to make another picture. He worked and worked, cutting and pasting. After perfecting it, he displayed his finished masterpiece—a slight orange bud still wrapped in green, just peeping above the ground.

I had expected another bright, bursting tulip and was thrilled with his subtle variation. Hearing my surprise at his creation, Joseph spoke in a voice brimming with joy, "When I grow up I still want to play with my kids and draw nice pictures just like I do now."

I am terribly remiss if I do nothing to protest the mongers of war who would rob our children of their future. When will mothers lift prayers of peace instead of feigning helplessness? When will mothers speak out vigorously against war, instead of meekly watching their sons become cannon fodder for the greed of superpowers?

Every person killed or injured in war has been carried and nourished by a woman. More than anyone else, mothers know the human cost of bringing forth life. Unless women devote themselves to peacemaking, they betray the children they've brought into being. Historian Arnold Toynbee said, "The mothers of America have still to go into action [against the militarism of the Pentagon], and I believe this is a battle that the Pentagon cannot win. In the mothers of America I do still see some hope for the world."[6]

"God did not give us a spirit of timidity, but a spirit of power, of love and of self-discipline" (2 Timothy 1:7).

It is true that power corrupts, but so does fatalistic timidity. Too many of us women have been irresponsible and frivolous with our use of time and conviction. We have been encouraged by our culture to remain infantile, not to change and grow. Too few of us are willing to take the risks involved in moving out, confronting evil, changing structures, demanding justice and peace.

Women are capable of adapting to the masculine world. Many have internalized the prevailing cultural values, thinking that power and dominance are of ultimate worth. Yet it isn't by developing "macho" skills that women can find fulfillment, but by reintroducing into modern Western civilization the sense of the person, the primacy of personal relationship so lacking among us today.[7]

Women, our mission is tenderness, not only in the nursery, but on other jobs as well. We have been instructed to hold tenderness in contempt, confusing it with softness or sentimentality. Tenderness, however, is attention to the person. If person-centered sensitivity and nurture were considered strong human values, instead of weak feminine traits, Hiroshima and Vietnam would not have happened.

Women, as the prime bearers of life, want the future to thrive. With our prayers and our writing, our prophetic word to power and our work in social services, at home and in the churches, we can become a decisive factor in the preservation of Mother Earth. With our commitment to ecological sanity, social justice, and simple living we can wreck the mechanistic madness of our society. We can bring our society home to the "reasons of the heart." Rightly understood, "self-sacrifice" and "service" are the last defense we have against a world wholly given over to profit and power.[8]

Robert Briffault said, "We live in a patriarchal society in which patriarchal principles have ceased to be valid.... Power, energy, ambition, intellect, the interests of the combative male, no more achieve fulfillment of his being than they can of themselves build up a human society."[9] The emulated heroes of our world have been victorious, saber-rattling, conquering males. We have not equally esteemed women and their strengths. Until we raise the status of women and value the "feminine" in all of us, we will be losing the battle to preserve life on our planet.

So-called "feminine" qualities such as compassion, intuition, endurance, and humaneness are a force capable of changing the world. We need women who acknowledge these qualities as strengths and are ready to be involved in a mission that extends beyond being a good wife and mother at home. We need men who will cultivate these qualities and care as much for their families as their careers. As members of "God's household" and chosen children of God's dearly loved family we are all invited (men and women) to clothe ourselves with "compassion, kindness, humility, gentleness and patience" (Colossians 3:12).

Every level of our society needs an exchange, a dialogue,

real collaboration between men and women if we are to bring about fundamental change in our cultural priorities. When women's opportunities for work reach parity with men's, and men's responsibility for child care reaches a parity with women's, the smallest unit of society—the family—should be considerably more gentle and humane. [10]

Centuries of parenting have called forth those compassionate qualities that we need more of in our society! As more and more adults share in parental responsibilities, the calculations of boardroom decisions will change; security will center around persons instead of defending systems!

The ultimate issue is how to move toward the creation of God's new community, where the barriers of prejudice and discrimination are destroyed. Those barriers can be replaced with mutually enriching relationships when the gifts of each individual are freed, in the new community, for use toward God's glory. The equality of male and female is grounded in the doctrine of the New Creation in Jesus Christ. When anyone is united to Christ there is a new world; the old order is gone, and a new order has already begun! Union with Christ moves us out of the old, fallen order where males dominated females, into a new order where we "are all one in Christ Jesus."

The church is very dear to me, but I am often hurt by its patriarchal mannerisms. The use of male-centered religious language reinforces and perpetuates the superiority of males and the inferiority of females. Though women do much of the day-to-day work of the church, the power structure is overwhelmingly male, and males do the important functions in the worship service. Why shouldn't women also minister? Ministry is such a nurturing job. Why shouldn't men teach children and cook the fellowship meals?

God is neither male nor female. God is both male and female. God is powerful, just, aggressive, but also compassionate, comforting, loving. God is a spirit and far above
the limitations of one sex or the other. Valuing the "female"
in each other and in God should lead to an improved status
of women in the churches.

It shouldn't surprise us that the Bible uses predominantly
masculine imagery for God, since the Bible was written
within a patriarchal context. What is surprising is the large
number of female images of God. Knowing that God's Holy
Spirit saw to it that references to God as female and
feminine were included in Scripture ought to empower
women to take on whatever spiritual leadership roles they
are gifted for. And they ought to enable men to accept and
honor the so-called feminine traits in themselves.[11]

Katie Funk Wiebe noted in a report on women's concerns
that her own Mennonite Brethren Church has made significant positive changes regarding women in the last ten years:

> 1. There is general strengthening of all women's structures,
> both formal and informal.
>
> 2. More young women are aware of feminist issues. More
> men are willing to find new kinds of marriage partnership.
>
> 3. More women are willing and ready to consider leadership
> roles.
>
> 4. More women are attending seminary and finding
> theology a resource for helping others.
>
> 5. We are all becoming more historically aware, thanks to
> publication of biographies of women and histories of
> women's activities in our churches.[12]

We can change! We can grow! We can turn all of history around if we have the will and a spirit of compassion that is determined to pull our world back from the brink of disaster. Such is the substance of hope.

Yet we have only just begun. "Rise up, O women of God! Have done with lesser things; give heart and soul and mind and strength to serve the King of kings."[13] Rise up, O women of God, to care courageously for your children, your husband, your church. Rise up to humanize your world lest it be destroyed by those who would exploit and abuse it for profit and for pride.

Our family began reading Bible stories regularly after the evening meal when Timothy was barely two. The message he gleaned from the Garden of Eden story was, "God said, 'No, no!' to the snake." For weeks after the rendition of that story, he would suddenly yell at the top of his lungs, "God said, 'No, no!' to the snake." I was reminded now of those theatrics as I meditated on Mary, the mother of Jesus. God said to the snake, "I will put enmity between you and the woman, and between your offspring and hers; *he will crush your head*, and you will strike his heel" (Genesis 3:15, italics added).

Mary, a simple handmaiden, understood that hidden deep within her was a message of hope for an aching world. God's resounding "NO!" would crush the snake forever. In the most ordinary and yet most miraculous event of birth, the Messiah, the Savior of the world was to be born.

> My soul praises the Lord
>   and my spirit rejoices in God my Savior,
> For he has been mindful of the humble
>   state of his servant.

From now on all generations will call me blessed. . . .
He has performed mighty deeds with his arm;
    he has scattered those who are proud in their inmost
    thoughts.
He has brought down rulers from their thrones
    but has lifted up the humble.
He has filled the hungry with good things
    but has sent the rich away empty.

—Luke 1:46-48, 51-53

Mary's obedience and words depict a world being turned
upside down. A humble woman of low estate claims God as
the liberator God who reverses the social order. Through
Mary, God is putting down the mighty and lifting up the
lowly. Through her offspring comes a new day, a new age!

Our offspring are not messiahs. Our babies will not be *the*
Savior of the world. Yet with Mary, in her Magnificat, we
are moved to magnify the one who has shown strength, scat-
tered the proud, and exalted those of low degree. We rejoice
in our children who endure as a sign of hope in a world of
despair. We trust that they will cherish and save our good
earth; that they will carry torches of light into the next
generation, dispelling gloom and confusion; that they will
endure as God's new gesture of good will toward all.

"Mama," asked Joseph, "will there always be wars in this
world?"

"Yes," I answered, "until God makes all things new."

"I wish there were no hurts in this world," he responded,
blinking back tears. "It makes me so sad when I think about
it."

I ache inside too. While driving through an elegant
suburban neighborhood, I observed the perfect lawns and
shrubbery, the white picket fences, the lace curtains, and the

cozy, well-lit living rooms. Oh for the freedom wholeheartedly to enjoy beauty and peace in the knowledge that
everyone the whole world over is privileged to enjoy the
same. Must I always ache inside? Then a passage from J. R.
R. Tolkien flitted into mind. It follows the ruin of the Dark
Lord and his evil minions:

> "A great Shadow has departed," said Gandalf, and then he
> laughed, and the sound was like music, or like water in a
> parched land; and as he listened the thought came to Sam [a
> hobbit] that he had not heard laughter, the pure sound of
> merriment, for days upon days without count. It fell upon
> his ears like the echo of all the joys he had ever known. But
> he himself burst into tears. Then, as a sweet rain will pass
> down a wind of spring and the sun will shine out the clearer,
> his tears ceased, and his laughter welled up, and laughing he
> sprang from his bed.
>
> *"How do I feel?"* he cried.... *"I feel like spring after
> winter, and sun on the leaves; and like trumpets and harps
> and all the songs I have ever heard!"*[14]

Why do gurgling babies, playful puppies, exquisite
flowers, and colorful birds stand there before us taunting us
with their perfection, while we labor under despair and
pain? Why are there such "stunning somethings" when
there could easily be nothing at all? When we come close to
despair over human stupidity; when the lakes and rivers are
turned into sewers; when the weapons stockpiles threaten us
with oblivion; when mothers and babies by the thousands
die every day for lack of bread, a mystery of good and
perfection offers a "maternal embrace."[15]

God's good creation surrounds us with hope that God
intended only good, and that God will again make life truly

good for every one of the Creator's children! Newness of life and its goodness are a gift from the Giver of good. Hope is a gift of the Spirit, a gift that, like laughter, can be contagious if we devote ourselves to its nurture.

The Mennonite Hymnal has a song which is infectiously joyful—"In Thee is gladness amid all sadness, Jesus, sunshine of my heart!" It continues:

> If He is ours
> We fear no powers,
> Nor of earth, nor sin, nor death;
> He sees and blesses
> In worst distresses,
> He can change them with a breath![16]

My child snuggled securely in my arms. "Are you taking care of me?" His eyes are filled with question.

"Yes, Mama and Daddy will take care of you, dear one. You are precious beyond reckoning and we *will* take care of you."

Little does he know how helpless we are to protect him from harm. Yet we have found a faith, a hope by which to live. Whether in pain, in danger, or in prosperity, we know that nothing—absolutely nothing—can separate us from the love of God. To be alive is to be vulnerable. To be born is to start traveling toward death. Childbirth is an affirmation of life, a rebuttal of death! Our children's presence, their spark of life, serve to taunt the futile efforts of those who would only destroy.

Jesus, when looking at Jerusalem, did not say, "Tut, tut, you deserve your impending destruction." No! He wept and said, "Would that even today you knew the things that make for peace."

The citizens of Jerusalem did not recognize the Prince of Peace among them, and as Jesus prophesied, they and their children were dashed to the ground. Perhaps in our generation, because of the enormity of impending doom, we will recognize that we have no security but the security of the Lord of the universe. Perhaps in our generation we will acknowledge the reign of our Lord God, the Prince of Peace.

"I have set before you life and death, blessings and curses. Now choose life, so that you and your children may live" (Deuteronomy 30:19).

It is truly unnerving to realize that those poised to push the nuclear button are elderly men with most of their lives behind them. What of the children with most of their lives still ahead? What of the young parents whose every waking moment is bent on equipping their children with the opportunity to live full, wholesome lives?

When the seige ramps were built against Jerusalem and sword, famine, and plague debilitated the city, Jeremiah wrote, "And though the city will be handed over to the Babylonians, you, O Sovereign Lord, say to me, 'Buy the field with silver and have the transaction witnessed.' "

Why? Because, "Once more fields will be bought in this land of which you say, 'It is a desolate waste. . . .' Fields will be bought for silver . . . because I will restore their fortunes, declares the Lord" (Jeremiah 32).

With the siege ramps built against our future, we have chosen life. We have chosen children as an affirmation of life. "Hope is found in massive outpourings of tiny, newborn cries."[17]

We have "no language but a cry"; a cry of protest against death; the cry of the Child who came to defeat death in all our tomorrows and to bring us together—mothers and fathers and children—into *one family of children.*

The whole creation has been groaning as in the pains of childbirth. And we ourselves, who have the firstfruits of the Spirit, groan inwardly as we wait eagerly for our adoption as sons and daughters of God.

Now if we are children, then we are heirs—heirs of God and coheirs with Christ. In Christ Jesus, the Liberator God, all of us—men, women, and children—become heir to the glorious freedom of the children of God.

Notes

Chapter 1

1. Adrienne Rich, *Of Woman Born* (New York: W. W. Norton, 1976), p. 11.
2. Grady and Hazel Cole, "Tramp on the Street" (New York: Dixie Music Publishing Co., 1940 and 1947).
3. Virginia Ramey Mollenkott, "Unlimiting God," *The Other Side*, November 1983, p. 13. My discussion of God's maternal characteristics is based on Mollenkott's insights.
4. Sharon Begley with John Carey, "How Human Life Begins," *Newsweek*, January 11, 1982, p. 36.
5. Paul Tournier, *The Gift of Feeling* (London: SCM Press Ltd., first published in English, 1981), p. 115.
6. William D. Marbach, "Building the Bionic Man," *Newsweek*, July 19, 1982, p. 35.
7. Michael Novak, "The Family Out of Favor," *Harpers*, April 1976, p. 43.
8. Rich, p. 13.
9. Rita Kramer, *In Defense of the Family* (New York: Basic Books, Inc., 1983), pp. 34, 35.
10. Ibid., p. 35.
11. Rich, p. 151.
12. Ibid.
13. Ibid., pp. 153-155.

Chapter 2

1. E. E. Cummings, *100 selected poems* (New York: Grove Press, 1923), p. 18.
2. Robin Morgan ed., *Sisterhood Is Powerful* (New York: Vintage Books, 1970), p. xxxii.

3. Thomas Merton, *New Seeds of Contemplation* (New York: New Directions Books, 1961), pp. 52, 56.

Chapter 3

1. Fyodor Dostoyevsky, *The Brothers Karamazov* (New York: New American Library, 1957), p. 699 (italics added).
2. Anne Keegan, "Old man dies alone but not friendless," *Chicago Tribune*, January 9, 1984, section 1, pp. 1, 2.
3. Novak, p. 38.
4. Ibid., p. 44.
5. Ibid., p. 39.
6. Gladys Hunt, *Ms. Means Myself* (Grand Rapids: Zondervan, 1972), p. 92.
7. Novak, p. 37.
8. John Scanzoni, "Family: Crisis or Change?" *The Christian Century*, August 12-19, 1981, pp. 795, 798.

Chapter 4

1. Scott Peck, *The Road Less Traveled* (New York: Simon and Schuster, 1978), pp. 90 and 140.
2. Dorothy van Woerkom, *The Queen Who Couldn't Bake Gingerbread* (New York: Knopf, 1975).
3. Paul K. Jewett, *Man as Male and Female* (Grand Rapids: Eerdmans, 1975), p. 24.
4. Ibid., p. 14.
5. Tournier, p. 131.
6. Reta Finger, "Ladders and Circles," *Daughters of Sarah*, Jan/Feb 1984, p. 5.
7. Virginia Ramey Mollenkott, *Women, Men and the Bible* (Nashville: Abingdon, 1977), pp. 23, 24.
8. Letha Scanzoni and Nancy Hardesty, *All We're Meant to Be* (Waco, Texas: Word Books, 1974), p. 31.

Chapter 5

1. William Blake, "Infant Sorrow," *The Portable Blake* (New York: Viking Press, 1946), p. 114. The poem is not quoted in its entirety.
2. Kramer, p. 201.
3. Sidney Cornelia Callahan, *The Working Mother* (New York: Macmillan, 1971), p. 26.
4. Arlene Rossen Cardozo, *Women at Home* (New York: Doubleday, Inc., 1976), pp. 6, 7.

Chapter 6

1. Emily Dickinson, "I'm nobody! Who are you?" *Poems by Emily Dickinson*

(Boston: Little, Brown and Company, 1945), p. 15.
2. Fynn, *Mister God, This Is Anna* (London: William Collins Sons, 1974), p. 71.
3. Scanzoni and Hardesty, p. 11.
4. Ibid., p. 144.
5. T. Berry Brazelton, M.D., *Infants and Mothers* (New York: A Merloyd Lawrence Book, 1969, Revised Ed. 1983), p. xxiii.
6. Catharine Reeve, "Ties," *Sunday, The Chicago Tribune Magazine*, May 13, 1984, p. 10.
7. Thomas Merton, *No Man Is an Island* (New York: Harcourt, Brace, 1955), p. 129 (italics added).

Chapter 7
1. Merton, *No Man Is an Island*, p. 133.
2. Angela Barron McBride, *The Growth and Development of Mothers* (New York: Harper and Row, 1973), pp. xiv, 32.
3. Bob Greene, *Good Morning, Merry Sunshine*, excerpted in the *Chicago Tribune*, June 17, 1984, section 2, pp. 1, 4.
4. Novak, p. 39.
5. Kramer, pp. 31, 32.
6. Cardozo, p. 6.
7. Callahan, p. 33.
8. Sandra Scarr, "What's a Parent to Do?" *Psychology Today*, May 1984, p. 61.
9. Selma Fraiberg, *Every Child's Birthright: In Defense of Mothering* (New York: Basic Books, 1977), pp. xi-xii.
10. Callahan, pp. 37-39.
11. Fraiberg, p. 64.
12. Kramer, p. 74.
13. Kathryn Lindskoog, *Up from Eden* (Elgin: David C. Cook, 1976), p. 45.
14. Peck, p. 15.
15. Tournier, p. 63.
16. Virginia Ramey Mollenkott, "You Shall Receive Power," in *Women and the Ministries of Christ*, Evangelical Women's Caucus Conference Publication, edited by Roberta Hestenes and Lois Curley (Pasadena: Fuller Theological Seminary, 1979), p. 112.

Chapter 8
1. Penelope Leach, *Babyhood* (New York: Penguin Books, 1974), p. 16.
2. Anna Bowman, "Woman and the Mennonite Patriarchy," article printed in the Goshen College Bulletin, March 1982.
3. Rich, pp. 21, 22.
4. Jane Lazarre, *The Mother Knot* (New York: McGraw-Hill, 1976), p. vii.
5. Janet Umble Reedy, "Beyond the Motherhood Mystique," in *Which Way Women?* edited by Dorothy Yoder Nyce (Akron, Pa.: MCC, Task Force on Women, 1980), p. 92.

6. Lindskoog, p. 37.
7. Novak, p. 42.
8. Lewis B. Smedes, *How Can It Be All Right When Everything Is All Wrong?* (New York: Harper and Row, 1982), p. 63.
9. " 'Tis the Gift to Be Simple," copyright, 1971, by Augsburg Publishing House.
10. Josephine Moffett Benton, *The Pace of a Hen* (Philadelphia: The Christian Education Press, 1961), p. 9.
11. Emily Dickinson, "Have you got a brook in your little heart?" *Poems by Emily Dickinson*, p. 130 (not quoted in its entirety).
12. Fynn, pp. 145-146.
13. Quoted in Ernest Boyer, "Edges and Rhythms," *Sojourners*, June 1982, p. 18.
14. Ibid., p. 19.

Chapter 9

1. William Blake, "The Little Boy Lost," p. 88.
2. Scarr, p. 61.
3. Brazelton, p. xxix.
4. Quoted from Lindskoog, p. 42.
5. Brazelton, p. xxvii.
6. Ibid.
7. "How Are Men Changing," *Newsweek*, January 16, 1978, p. 45.
8. Ibid.
9. Ibid., p. 41.
10. Quoted in Kari Torjesen Malcolm, *Women at the Crossroads* (Downers Grove, Ill.: InterVarsity Press, 1982), p. 158.
11. Mollenkott, *Women, Men and the Bible*, p. 32.
12. Diane L. MacDonald, "Jesus and Women," in *Which Way Women*, p. 10.
13. Mollenkott, "You Shall Receive Power," pp. 111, 112.
14. Elisabeth Schüssler Fiorenza, "Feminist Spirituality, Christian Identity, and Catholic Vision," in Carol P. Christ and Judith Plaskow, *Womanspirit Rising: A Feminist Reader in Religion* (San Francisco: Harper and Row, 1979), p. 137.
15. Roberta Hestenes, "Culture, Counter-culture and Christian Transformation," in *Women and the Ministries of Christ*, p. 281.
16. Willard Krabill, "Creating Our Destiny—in Human Sexuality," in *Which Way Women*, p. 32.
17. Quoted in Lindskoog, p. 25.
18. Quoted in McBride, p. 146.

Chapter 10

1. Matthew Arnold, "The Buried Life," in *The Poetical Works of Matthew Arnold* (New York: Thomas Y. Crowell Co., 1897), pp. 284-285. The poem is not quoted in its entirety.
2. Mollenkott, *Women, Men and the Bible*, p. 119.
3. Cited in McBride, pp. 137, 138.

4. John Alexander, "Feminism as a Subversive Activity," in *The Other Side*, July 1982, p. 8.
5. Reta Finger, "One-Sided Submission," in *Sojourners*, September 1981, p. 33.
6. Rosemary Radford Reuther, "Of One Humanity," *Sojourners*, January 1984, p. 19.
7. Pamela Laber, "Our children: myth and reality," *Chicago Tribune*, June 6, 1984, section 1, p. 15.
8. Fraiberg, pp. 123, 124.
9. Anne Bowen Follis, *"I'm Not a Women's Libber, But ..."* (Nashville: Abingdon, 1981), p. 46.
10. Ibid., pp. 25, 27.
11. Laber, p. 15.
12. Follis, p. 58.
13. Above discussion taken from Ruth C. Stoltzfus, "Family Violence: A Look at Our Common Ground Against a Common Problem," in *Which Way Women?* p. 42.
14. Callahan, p. 30.
15. Scarr, p. 60.
16. Quoted in McBride, p. 134.
17. Cited in Callahan, p. 26.
18. Quoted from Valerie Saiving, in Carmody, p. 50.

Chapter 11

1. Blake, "Holy Thursday," p. 101. This poem is not quoted in its entirety.
2. Philip Hallie, *Lest Innocent Blood Be Shed* (New York: Harper and Row, 1979), p. 274.
3. Ibid.
4. C. S. Lewis, *The Weight of Glory* (Grand Rapids: Eerdmans, 1965), p. 15.
5. Mary Evelyn Jegen, "Women and World Hunger," in *Which Way Women?* p. 51.
6. Denise Lardner Carmody, *Feminism and Christianity: A Two-Way Reflection* (Nashville: Abingdon, 1982), p. 153.
7. Quoted from the New Internationalist in *Women and the Ministries of Christ*, p. 217.
8. Susan Hill Lindley, "Feminist Theology in a Global Perspective," in *Which Way Women?* p. 69.
9. Jegen, p. 51.
10. Raymond Fung, "Come to the Table," *The Other Side*, November 1982, p. 11.
11. Jegen, p. 54.
12. Fung, p. 11.
13. Ibid., p. 13.
14. Elizabeth Stark, "The Unspeakable Family Secret," *Psychology Today*, May 1984, p. 42.
15. Lindskoog, p. 38.
16. Dostoyevsky, pp. 224-226.

17. Quoted in Laber, p. 15.
18. Fraiberg, pp. 111, 133.
19. Brazelton, p. xxv.
20. Scanzoni, p. 795.
21. Laber, p. 15.

Chapter 12

1. Joe Pearson, "Children all," in *Children: Of Such Is the Kingdom*, (Independence, Mo.: Herald House, 1979).
2. Fynn, p. 71.
3. Oscar Wilde, *The Selfish Giant* (New York: Methuen, 1978).
4. John F. Alexander, "Fantasy," *The Other Side*, December 1983, pp. 6, 7.
5. Henri Nouwen, "The Selfless Way of Christ," *Sojourners*, June 1981, p. 14.
6. e e cummings, p. 114 (not quoted in its entirety).
7. Fynn, p. 12.
8. Virginia Master-Johnson in *Tempo, Chicago Tribune*, November 17, 1983.
9. Thornton Wilder, *Our Town* (New York: Harper and Row, 1938), pp. 99, 100.
10. Gladys Hunt, *Honey for a Child's Heart* (Grand Rapids: Zondervan, 1969), p. 112.
11. Emily Dickinson, "He ate and drank the precious words," *Poems by Emily Dickinson*, p. 13.
12. Quoted in David Kahn, "The Anatomy of Unselfish Love," n.d.
13. Ibid.
14. Merton, *No Man Is an Island*, p. 19.

Chapter 13

1. Alfred Tennyson, *The Complete Poetical Works of Tennyson* (Cambridge, Mass.: Riverside Press, 1898), excerpt from "In Memoriam," pp. 175, 176.
2. Quoted in Hedy Sawadsky, "Peacemaking in Colorado," in *Which Way Women?* pp. 152, 153.
3. Quoted in Sawadsky, p. 151.
4. Jim Wallis, "Living in Hope," *Sojourners*, April 1984, p. 4.
5. Ibid.
6. Quoted in Donald D. Kaufman, "Mothers work for peace," *Gospel Herald*, May 4, 1982, p. 309.
7. Tournier, p. 5.
8. Carmody, p. 139.
9. Robert Briffault, quoted in Rich, p. 90.
10. Carmody, p. 118.
11. Mollenkott, "Unlimiting God," p. 12.
12. Katie Funk Wiebe, "Ten Years Later," from MCC Committee on Women's Concerns *Report*, July-August 1983, p. 5.
13. William Pierson Merrill, "Rise Up, O Men of God," 1911, *The Mennonite*

Hymnal (Scottdale, Pa.: Herald Press, 1969). For emphasis I replaced "men" with "women."

14. J. R. R. Tolkien, *The Return of the King* (New York: Ballantine Books, 1965), p. 283 (italics added).

15. Carmody, p. 159.

16. Johann Lindemann, c. 1595, Tr. Catherine Winkworth, 1858, "In Thee Is Gladness," *The Mennonite Hymnal*.

17. Joyce Hollyday, "euclid street journal," *Sojourners*, September 1982, p. 25.

Ronald Sider

EXPLORING THE LIMITS OF NON-VIOLENCE

'There are only two invincible forces in the twentieth century – the atom bomb and non-violence.' *Bishop Leonidas Proano of Ecuador*

'What good would it do for three kayaks, three canoes and a rubber dinghy to paddle into the path of a Pakistani steamship?' asks Ron Sider. 'Or for an eighty-year-old lady in a wheelchair to stop in front of advancing Filipino tanks?' These are examples of some of the remarkable victories of non-violent campaigns in recent years that Ron Sider documents as he considers the likelihood such campaigns have of ever achieving substantial results.

'How can Christians in the just war tradition claim that the violence they justify is truly a last resort until they have tried the non-violent alternative?' asks Sider. In answer, he details strong biblical justification for non-violence, and offers suggestions for putting these principles into practice.

Penelope Smith

ALL THE DAYS OF MY LIFE

'I admire the skill and innate wisdom with which she interweaves the real with the more-than-real. She has managed to give another dimension to the problems that beset our age. God knows we need a perspective such as hers.'

Mary Craig

Written during her third pregnancy, *All the Days of My Life* is a profound autobiography of originality and charm in which Penelope Flint's own growing spiritual awareness mirrors the growth of the child within. It culminates in the seventh month of pregnancy, with her acceptance as an external candidate to St Mary's Convent, Wantage – a symbolic confirmation of an inner process which had begun in her days studying English at Oxford.

Interspersed with Penelope Flint's own startling poetry, *All the Days of My Life* is a vivid account of the inner and outer life of a woman searching for an authentic spiritual reality. It affirms that space for reflection and growth can and must be found amidst the pressures of everyday life. The author's knowledge of philosophical and Christian writings, and her understanding of current affairs enhance this outstanding book.

SPIRE

Rebecca de Saintonge

OUTSIDE THE GATE

Nico Smith shocked many people when as a white man with an impeccable Afrikaner pedigree, a prestigious university job and a comfortable home, he moved house with his wife Ellen to the deprived and despised South African township of Mamelodi.

Born into a staunchly Afrikaner family, Nico Smith had been taught to regard black people as an inferior race. But at the height of his career his doubts began. How could he, as a Christian theologian, reconcile the policies of apartheid with the Gospel's command to 'love your neighbour as yourself'?

This vivid biography charts Nico Smith's painful and courageous pilgrimage for justice, which cost him friends, status and respectability. It also explores the relationship between Christianity and politics, the witness of the church in a volatile society, and the reasons for the divisions and prejudices in South Africa today. Mamelodi is now a major centre for the reconciliation of whites and blacks, where Nico Smith and his friends work out what it means to identify with the shame of Christ's crucifixion, and join Him 'outside the gate'.

SPIRE

Elizabeth Goudge

A BOOK OF FAITH

'The compiling of an anthology can be an act of thanks-giving. What would any of us do without the books and poems that help us along our way? – the books we return to again and again, the poems we learn by heart and repeat for comfort in sleepless nights?' *Elizabeth Goudge*

Elizabeth Goudge is known and loved the world over for her gentle, absorbing writing. An avid reader herself, she brought together her favourite poems and prose passages in this classic collection on the subject of faith, including selections from the Bible, George Herbert, Julian of Norwich, George Macdonald, Norman Nicholson, Rainer Marie Rilke, Helen Waddell, James Kirkup, Leo Tolstoy, Geoffrey Grigson, Gerard Manley Hopkins and the nuns of Burnham Abbey.

A Book of Faith will be turned to in moments of stress and in times of reflection. Elizabeth Goudge brought taste, love and her own profound faith to this collection, which offers the precious gift of serenity to all its readers. Fully indexed, it is ideal for personal use or as a gift.

SPIRE